30 Days
to
Spiritual Health

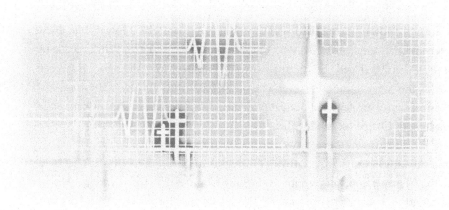

Dan & Tim Riordan

 GreenTree Publishers
www.greentreepublishers.com
Newnan, GA

30 Days to Spiritual Health

Copyright © 2022 by Timothy Riordan

All rights reserved. No part of this publication may be reproduced, stored in a retrieval system, or transmitted by any means – electronic, mechanical, photographic (photocopying), recording, or otherwise – without prior permission in writing from the author.

Unless otherwise noted, Scripture taken from the NEW AMERICAN STANDARD BIBLE®, Copyright © 1960, 1962, 1963, 1968, 1971, 1972, 1973, 1975, 1977, 1995 by The Lockman Foundation. Used by permission. (www.Lockman.org)

Scripture quotations marked (NIV) are taken from the Holy Bible, New International Version®, NIV®. Copyright © 1973, 1978, 1984, 2011 by Biblica, Inc.™ Used by permission of Zondervan. All rights reserved worldwide. www.zondervan.comThe "NIV" and "New International Version" are trademarks registered in the United States Patent and Trademark Office by Biblica, Inc.™

Scripture quotations marked (NLT) are taken from the Holy Bible, New Living Translation, copyright ©1996, 2004, 2015 by Tyndale House Foundation. Used by permission of Tyndale House Publishers, Carol Stream, Illinois 60188. All rights reserved.

Printed in the United States of America
ISBN-13: 978-1-944483-52-4

Follow Dr. Tim Riordan through the following media links:
Website/blog: timriordan.com
Twitter: @tim_riordan
Greentree Publishers
Greentreepublishers.com

Cover graphic credits:
Shutterstock.com – GD Arts

Gift Offer...

Thank you for choosing Dan and Tim Riordan's *30 Days to Spiritual Health*. We hope this book will be a blessing to you and your church.

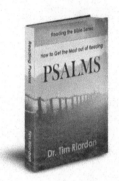

We are offering the digital version of Dr. Tim Riordan's book, *How to Get the Most out of Reading Psalms*, as a thank you gift. You will find this to be a useful companion to his other book on Psalms: *Songs from the Heart: Meeting with God in the Psalms*. To receive your pdf copy, please visit
Greentreepublishers.com/free-gift---psalms.html.
This book is not available through retail stores.

Are you willing to write a brief review?

We would also like to ask up front if you would be so kind as to write a review of this book on Amazon and/or your favorite retailer. Reviews will help future readers to be blessed by this helpful resource. We pray you enjoy your 30-Day Journey, and we trust God will use this time to enrich your life.

GreenTree Publishers

Contents

Beginnings

In my twenties, I hiked a little of the Appalachian Trail in Georgia and decided if I section-hiked it, I would eventually complete the whole 2200-mile trail. I didn't realize hiking forty or fifty miles a year would take forever to finish, so somewhere in Virginia, I committed to completing at least 100 miles a year. I've now increased my mileage to 200 miles because I don't want to be climbing Mt. Katahdin with a walker.

Backpacking has taught me wonderful lessons about life, but one of the most important lessons has been life is a journey filled with ups and downs, victories and defeats. That's been true in my life as a husband, father, pastor, and writer. I've experienced this truth in my spiritual life as well.

Yes, life is a journey.

You are about to begin an incredible, thirty-day journey toward spiritual health. Dan and I created this devotional to help you encounter God in fresh ways on your journey toward Christlikeness and spiritual health. You may also be working through this book as a part of a church health campaign your church family is experiencing.

Whether you are using this devotional individually or with others, we want you to consider the health characteristics of your church. A spiritually healthy church is made up of spiritually healthy Christians. How will you contribute toward making your church a healthy church?

We are all familiar with the consequences of getting a virus and passing it on to others. Spiritual infection can happen the same way. If one Christian has a bad attitude or relationship problem that has grown into bitterness, that bitterness will not be contained. It can, and usually does, spread easily through the church. If your church is using the Natural Church Development profile, this infection would show up as a low score in the characteristic of *loving relationships.*

Whether or not you are using the profile, we hope you will consider how your health, or unhealthiness, affects your entire church. Think about attitudes or practices that may make your church unhealthy. If you're using the profile, review scores showing the minimum factor of church health and look for ways to improve that quality through your actions and commitments. Ask God to direct you through this process to show how you can influence others to make similar adjustments so your church family can be strong and effective in fulfilling its mission. If you are using this book individually or corporately as a church, we want this journey to be exciting, life-changing, and fruitful.

Just as my excursions through the mountains are filled with adventure and memorable encounters with God through nature, the journey you are about to begin will also be exciting and inspiring as you discover new thoughts about God and yourself. The journey, however, is not easy; it will take commitment.

You may have a daily quiet time during which, through prayer and Bible study, you meet with God. If you don't, now's a good time to start. This devotional will offer daily scripture, opportunities for personal reflection, a guide for prayer, and points of personal application.

Although the journey will include Bible study, we want to emphasize meeting with God through Scripture *and* prayer. Prayer is an integral part of spiritual health and life-change as we follow Jesus. We encourage you not to rush through this book but to go slowly in order to experience the journey. When we ask you to reflect on a Bible verse, take time to do so. When we suggest you stop and pray about a matter, do it then. We may ask you to share a thought or experience with a friend. Take time at that moment and decide whom you'll call or meet to tell them about your discovery.

Several things will help you on this journey. It's like putting the right equipment in your pack so you won't go into the wilderness and miss the enjoyment and life-change possible through your encounter with God.

Your Bible will be a vital part of the journey. Throughout this book, we'll suggest Bible memory verses as theme scriptures. People tend to think Scripture memory is for children, but it's for everyone. Psalm 119:11 says, "I have hidden Your Word in my heart that I might not sin against You." Take time to memorize the scripture. You may want to write it on a card and carry it with you throughout your day. Use it in conversation and talk about it with your spouse, friends, and children.

Sometimes when I'm reading a book and the author mentions a familiar passage, I think to myself, "I know that verse," and I quickly move past it. Don't do that! I've tried to stop missing out on new nuggets of truth God may want to share through familiar verses.

Hebrews 4:12

"For the word of God is living and active and sharper than any two-edged sword, and piercing as far as the division of soul and spirit, of both joints and marrow, and able to judge the thoughts and intentions of the heart."

Take a moment to read the Bible verse in the box. Don't move past this familiar scripture. God may have a fresh word for you.

What does this verse mean when it says God's Word is living and active? Go ahead. Write out your thoughts. Writing helps cement truths into your heart and leads to application.

_____

_____

_____

You might use something sharp to cut packages open. In this case, God's Word will cut open your heart, soul, and mind. It will help you discern truth and recognize when you embrace a lie. Sometimes, this cutting process is painful. Can you think of a time when reading God's Word has cut you open and revealed something in the deep places of your life? Write a few sentences explaining that experience.

_____

_____

_____

One essential resource you'll need on the journey is time. I know it's hard to fit time into your pack, but you have to do it. I have had so many ambitions but never got around to doing them. My accomplishments came because of planning.

You'll need a block of time every day to read, pray, and reflect. It could be fifteen minutes or so, or you may want to spend additional time on each day's reading. I think it's best to start my day with a quiet time, but some people choose to do it during lunch or other times. When is a good time for you to meet with God on this journey? Write it in the space below.

_____

Another crucial part of your prayer journey is a journal. If you don't have a prayer and Christian life journal, you can get a small notebook and create your own.

We suggest you take time each day before you begin reading to pray about your day and ask God to prepare your heart for whatever He may want to show you. As you're reading the devotion, stop and pray as you feel led about the things you're reading.

Stop reading now and ask God to guide you on this journey. Commit yourself to the task of reading daily and meeting with God.

We also suggest you include a partner on your journey. It's best to include your spouse if you're married. If not, find a friend who will join you. Who is someone you can ask? Write his or her name in the space below.

___*Jimmy or Barbara*___

Additional partners you can include on your journey might be the people in your small group or Sunday School class. Your experience in *30 Days to Spiritual Health* will be improved if you regularly involve your small group. Talk about your experiences and pray together about issues found in this devotional.

We divide this devotional into various parts. The first part focuses primarily on prayer and encountering God. The second part will lead you to think about growth principles Christian Schwarz of Natural Church Development called *Growth Forces*.

The final section focuses on eight quality characteristics that will lead to healthy Christians and healthy churches. We'll spend two days on each growth characteristic in the last section. We'll focus on a different word of the characteristic each day.

I'm so excited you are joining us for this journey. We are praying for you even if we don't know you by name. We want God to meet with you on this journey and take you to a new place of spiritual fruit, growth, and health.

Hopefully, you have your pack ready to begin the journey. God is looking forward to meeting with you.

Scripture Memory Verse

John 17:3 This is eternal life, that they may know You, the only true God, and Jesus Christ whom You have sent.

Day One

Knowing God

"Show me Your glory." That passage in Exodus 33 came to mind as I climbed to the vista atop a Virginia mountain called "The Priest." I stood transfixed in front of one of the most glorious, indescribable views I've ever beheld. I felt as if I was looking into the face of God.

yes   Seeing

Have you ever had such an experience? *yes* An experience that prompted you to think you had a close encounter with the Divine?

Moses had that experience, and Exodus 33 records it. It's a fantastic story. After the fiasco of the golden calf, God told Moses He would send an angel to lead them to the Promised Land, and they were to pack up and leave Mt. Horeb. God said He would not go with them because of their obstinance, but He would make sure they arrived safely.

The people were heartbroken over their sin and God's refusal to go with them. Read Exodus 33:13-15 in the box and look at part of Moses' reply to God's statement.

What was Moses' first desire?

He wanted to know God's ways

> **Exodus 33:13-15**
>
> "Now therefore, I pray You, if I have found favor in Your sight, let me know Your ways that I may know You, so that I may find favor in Your sight. Consider too, that this nation is Your people." [14] And He said, "My presence shall go *with you,* and I will give you rest." [15] Then he said to Him, "If Your presence does not go *with us,* do not lead us up from here."

In verse twelve, Moses quoted God saying, "I have known you by name," so is it any wonder Moses desired to know God? Why did Moses want to know God? Look again at the verse and write your response below.

He wanted to have his favor — He also said he wouldn't go unless God went with them

Moses understood the way to find favor with God was to *know* Him. Several things come to mind from this encounter. One is God is knowable! This powerful truth is the heartbeat of our faith. God wants a relationship with us and has bridged the chasm between us through Jesus Christ to make that relationship possible.

Another thing that gets my attention in this passage is Moses told God he and the Israelites didn't want to go to the Promised Land if God wasn't going with them. Wow! God had just described this land as "flowing with milk and honey," but Moses said God was more valuable. They had just spent many years as slaves in Egypt and were finally free, only to wander in the wilderness. Now, they had the opportunity to have a permanent home, but Moses said God was more valuable and refused to move forward.

John Ortberg once wrote, "It's like Moses said, 'I'd rather live in the wilderness with You than in the Promised Land without You.'" Can you make a statement like that? Honestly? What would living in the wilderness look like for you? Think about your life and what living the rest of your days in difficulty might reflect. Are you willing to say knowing God and experiencing God are more valuable than a life of ease? Than a life flowing with milk and honey?

Because God has given us His Word and the teachings found in the Bible, we realize God is knowable. The question may be how badly do we want to know Him? Look over Moses' prayer again in Exodus 33:13 and take a few moments to pray it back to God as your prayer. Are you willing to tell God that knowing Him is your greatest value? It's His.

In Exodus 33:18, Moses finally asks to see God's glory. What do you think of when you consider His glory? What does His glory mean? When we think of the glory of God, we think of the splendor and majesty of God, and rightly so. But it means much more. I heard someone say God's glory is what God is, all of His attributes and greatness.

The most common Old Testament word translated as glory means "weight" or "heaviness," while the most frequent New

Testament word focuses on radiance and brilliance. The glory of God points to the full expression or weight of God's identity as He shines brilliantly to those who desire to know Him.

Read how God described His glory in Exodus 33:19. You can see some words in His description of the full expression of the weight of His identity.

Back to Moses. God finally told Moses He would show His glory to him. He said Moses would not be able to view His face, so He would hide Moses in the cleft of a rock and cover him with His hand when He passed by.

Read Exodus 34:6-8 for a description of this encounter between Moses and God. Looking at these verses, how does God describe Himself to Moses?

compassionate,
gracious, slow to
anger etc.

We encounter God's glory through His goodness, grace, and compassion. He is slow to anger and overflowing with love and truth. He is also just. We don't have to climb a mountain to encounter God's glory. We experience His glory by knowing

Exodus 33:19

And He said, "I Myself will make all My goodness pass before you, and will proclaim the name of the Lord before you; and I will be gracious to whom I will be gracious, and will show compassion on whom I will show compassion."

Exodus 34:6-8

Then the Lord passed by in front of him and proclaimed, "The Lord, the Lord God, compassionate and gracious, slow to anger, and abounding in lovingkindness and truth; [7] who keeps lovingkindness for thousands, who forgives iniquity, transgression and sin; yet He will by no means leave the guilty unpunished, visiting the iniquity of fathers on the children and on the grandchildren to the third and fourth generations." [8] Moses made haste to bow low toward the earth and worship.

Him personally. Just like Moses, we need a passion to know God, and when we're consumed with that passion, God will pass by, and you will experience His majesty and glory.

Personal Reflection:
- On a scale of one to five, with five being the greatest, how would you rate your desire to know God?   *3*
- Are you willing to tell God you would give up everything to know Him? Would you rather live in challenging circumstances in this life with Him than in a life of ease without Him? *3*
- Spend a few moments in prayer communicating your desire to know God. If you struggle with making this desire the priority of your life, be honest with God. Tell Him you are willing to go on a journey with Him that will create in you a hunger for His glory.
- Confess any sin to Him that comes to mind. This sin can hinder godly desires that lead to a personal encounter with the Divine.
- Write a prayer in the space below that expresses your passion for knowing God.

Encountering God

When Dan and I were young, we fought. I know; fighting is terrible, but it's also normal. Dan is four years older than me, so he could have squashed me like a cockroach if he'd wanted. His method was not nearly as lethal but maybe a bit more humiliating. He'd hold me away by putting his hand on my head, and my arms weren't long enough to reach him. Then, he'd throw me on the ground and sit on me until I promised to quit fighting. I always promised, but we were at it again when he let me up.

Have you ever wrestled with someone and refused to give up? Have you ever wrestled with God?

If you have, you're in good company. Does anyone in the Bible come to mind when you think of wrestling with God? You're right—Jacob.

Before considering that famous wrestling match, which is a little hard to comprehend, let's go back into Jacob's life. Jacob's name means "heel grabber," for he held onto his twin brother's heel when he was born. The name is also an idiom for "one who betrays or deceives." Jacob was not a choir boy whom everyone recognized for his outstanding integrity. You probably remember how he deceived his father

Genesis 28:12-15

He had a dream, and behold, a ladder was set on the earth with its top reaching to heaven; and behold, the angels of God were ascending and descending on it. 13 And behold, the Lord stood above it and said, "I am the Lord, the God of your father Abraham... the land on which you lie, I will give it to you and to your descendants...15 Behold, I am with you and will keep you wherever you go, and will bring you back to this land; for I will not leave you until I have done what I have promised you."

and stole the birthright from his brother, Esau. Then, he had to flee for his life.

While running from Esau, Jacob had a dream in which he encountered God. You may want to read the entire dream recorded in Genesis 28:12-16 or look at the selected verses in the box.

Jacob awoke stunned. Using a rock as a pillow may not have helped, but he'd encountered the God of the universe—YAHWEH! In verse sixteen, he said, "Surely the Lord is in this place, and I did not know it." He used the Hebrew word for God's personal and most holy name, YAHWEH. God is in this place.

Imagine Jacob the Deceiver having an encounter with God. Surely, God could have found a worthier person. Think about the fact that Jacob met God. What does this meeting say to you about people encountering God?

_____

_____

You could have answered many ways, but your answer probably had to do with God's grace. God encounters come because God desires them.

What does that truth say to you and me? It says God wants encounters with us. Isn't that thought incredible?

Here's another stunning thought from this story. Jacob had an encounter with God and didn't recognize it at first. When we connect the truth of God's desire that we meet Him with the reality of His omnipresence (God is everywhere), God encounters may be more prolific than we realize.

Have you ever had an encounter with God? Write a little summary of that encounter below.

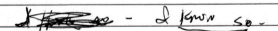

Have you had an encounter with God and not known it? Probably.

Probably

Here's another interesting thought about the dream we call "Jacob's Ladder." What was the purpose of the ladder? Was it for Jacob to reach up to God or for God to reach down to him? What do you think?

_____

Remember, God is always the initiator of an encounter, and He's probably taken the initiative in your life a lot!

You'd think this experience radically changed Jacob's life. Not really. At first, he was frightened and gave that place a memorable name, but he moved on with his life in the same self-centered manner. It's easy for us to do the same. Have you ever had a "God moment" only to go back to life as normal a short time later?

Jacob did.

Now, fast forward twenty years. Jacob worked fourteen years to earn the right to have Rachel as his wife. Laban, his father-in-law, deceived Jacob the Deceiver by tricking him into marrying Leah.

Leah was the oldest daughter and probably cross-eyed. Her name means cow (maybe even cow-face) or weary, but I have good news for those of you named Leah: it also means "delicate."

As Jacob began to lead his massive family back to Canaan, he knew he'd encounter an angry Esau. He schemed to get his brother's sympathy, which we read about in Genesis 32:1-23.

Verse twenty-four begins, "Then when Jacob was left alone..." When Jacob was left alone, he had an encounter with God that turned into a wrestling match that ended with Jacob being crippled, his name being changed to Israel, and God blessing him.

What is the significance of Jacob being alone and wrestling with God? Write your thoughts below. *God wanted to change Jacob*

_____

Do you think Jacob was wrestling with God as if Jacob might actually win? God could have disintegrated Jacob with a breath. This whole encounter wasn't about Jacob wrestling with God but about him wrestling with himself.

You could make a list of truths to draw from this story. Write some down in your journal. You may include something such as Jacob's encounter with God and blessing ending with pain. Coming to terms with God is sometimes painful.

Does God want to involve you in a wrestling match so you can find joy through pain? Are you experiencing that pain now? Have you ever experienced it?

Genesis 32:26-28

Then he said, "Let me go, for the dawn is breaking." But he said, "I will not let you go unless you bless me." 27 So he said to him, "What is your name?" And he said, "Jacob." 28 He said, "Your name shall no longer be Jacob, but Israel; for you have striven with God and with men and have prevailed."

Read Genesis 32:26-28. Did Jacob have God in a pinch? No. God's desire was for this encounter to end with a blessing, a mark that changed Jacob's life, and a name that changed his destiny.

Isn't that an incredible story? Jacob the Deceiver became Jacob the God-wrestler. He went from loser to winner, from zero to hero.

What must you do to recognize God is present in your life? Make a list of actions or activities you can do that lead to a greater awareness of His presence.

_____

_____

The omnipresent God has an encounter scheduled for you. Don't miss it. It may come in the middle of the night or in the depths of a personal battle. Watch for Him. Anticipate Him. He wants to change your life. *I want Him to change my life*

Personal Reflection

- Do you think God has ever initiated a meeting with you, and you turned a blind eye? Take a moment to confess your sin of

God if you initiate a meeting with me Help me to KNOW about it & help me realize it

Help me

callousness and tell God you want to live with your spiritual eyes fully open to His presence.

- Look at your list of actions that lead to a greater awareness of God's presence. Pick one you will put into practice today and do it.

- Do you think it's significant that Jacob's blessing came with the cost of pain? Are you willing to go through pain to meet with God and for God to change your life?

- Write a prayer below to express your desire to experience God. Share with God your passion and how far you're willing to go to encounter Him.

I help me to be willing to go through pain to meet with God

Forgive me when I love your word & I don't listen

Day Three

Right With God

What's the greatest scandal of all time? We've seen some doozies in the last few years. Some have made you scratch your head, while others have probably made you sick to your stomach. Imagine a scandal where a powerful political leader has an affair with a woman who ends up pregnant. Horrid, right?

It gets worse.

To cover his crime, the leader has the woman's husband murdered in a way that looks like a war casualty and quickly marries the grieving widow.

Sounds like something you'd read in one of those checkout counter newspapers at the grocery store. However, you can also find it in the Bible.

You have probably figured out I'm referring to King David and his affair with Bathsheba. The Bible puts all the blame on David, so we can only assume Bathsheba was innocent. David buried his sins of lust, adultery, and murder until the prophet Nathan confronted him. One of the harshest lines in the Bible is in 2 Samuel 12:7, when Nathan reveals that David is the sinner. "You are the man!" he tells David. You can read the whole encounter beginning in 2 Samuel 12:1, where

> **2 Samuel 12:9**
> "Why have you despised the word of the Lord by doing evil in His sight? You have struck down Uriah the Hittite with the sword, have taken his wife to be your wife, and have killed him with the sword of the sons of Ammon."

Nathan tells David the story of a rich man stealing the one little lamb of a poor man. Of course, the story exposes David's sin. Look at Nathan's strong rebuke in 2 Samuel 12:9.

How did Nathan characterize David's sin?

doing evil

It's easy for me to read that story and get in Nathan's corner. "Let him have it, Nathan." David's sin is repulsive and hard to believe. I can see adultery and murder as evil and as despising the Word of the Lord. The problem I have is that I can't get away from the four pungent words of the prophet: "You are the man!"

I can't get away from them because he spoke those words to me as well. Now, when God deals with sins, such as adultery, murder, and drunkenness, I'm in the "amen corner." When God starts to deal with the "lighter side" of transgression, like anger, greed, and unhealthy habits, I join ranks with the "Oh me" crowd, not to mention feeling like God's meddling by making little sins look bigger than they are.

Is He? Is He making sin look bigger than it is? No!

Our problem is we tend not to view sin from God's perspective, and we become personally offended when someone suggests our actions are less than admirable. Many in our society reject the idea that humanity is sinful and question whether anyone has the right to call something sin. Does anyone have that right? Yes, God does. Sin at its very core is rebellion against God, and everyone is guilty. We categorize sin because it makes us look less offensive, but God doesn't grade on a curve. What do you think Nathan meant when he said David had despised the Word of the Lord?

A sin is a sin? David didn't think what what he did was a sin!

Since all sin is rebellion against the Creator, it comes in response to the fact that we have turned a blind eye to the commands of the Lord. It doesn't matter what label we put on the action. If it's rebellion, it's sin. If it's ignoring God's commands, it's sin.

We all have a problem with sin. Ephesians 2:3 says we are "by nature children of wrath." It's probably a topic for another time, but the Bible has a lot to say about God's wrath. The fact is we are sinners, falling short of the glory of God. We didn't just miss the target a little; we were aiming in the wrong direction.

Being in a right relationship with God has two perspectives. One establishes our eternal standing with Him, and the other impacts our daily victory with Him. The first results in justification, and the second results in being set apart for God's purposes and enjoying abundant life and eternal fruit. A Bible word would be sanctification.

Being right with God first requires repentance of sin and submission to Christ as Lord. We won't truly repent of our sin unless we see it from God's perspective. David's sin is not the only sin considered scandalous and horrid. Yours and mine are too.

Repentance and faith leads to our salvation, our right standing with God. Have you done that? You may want to turn to the back of this book and review the section on how to become a Christian. Peter described our salvation in 1 Peter 1:3-4 as being "born again to a living hope." Do you have that living hope?

Even though Christians are right with God in terms of being made just through repentance and faith, believers still sin and hurt their fellowship with God and other believers. It also reduces spiritual fruit and health.

Even as Christians, we must make daily decisions not to despise the Word of the Lord and to forsake evil. Are you making these decisions?

In 1 Peter 1:16, we're reminded we should be holy just like God is holy. What does it mean to be holy?

_____

_____

1 Peter 1:15-16

But like the Holy One who called you, be holy yourselves also in all your behavior; [16] because it is written, "You shall be holy, for I am holy."

Holy means set apart. As Christians, we make daily choices that reflect our spiritual commitment to Christ to obey His Word and forsake evil. When we fail to obey Him, God calls us to confess our sin. Confessing our sin is agreeing with God that what we have done does not reflect His character and our commitment to being Christ-followers.

One passage that offers a great model as a prayer of confession is King David's prayer found in Psalm 51. Most scholars think David wrote this psalm after being confronted by Nathan. Read Psalm 51 in your Bible and think about how you can use those words as your expression of confession and repentance.

Make a list of God's characteristics described in Psalm 51:

loving kindness, tender mercy, rightness, cleanlyness for us —

Next, write down words found in the text that express your desire for repentance and renewal. The first is a request for God's grace. Verse one ends with a request for God to "blot out my transgressions." What other expressions communicate your desire to be right with God?

God I pray that you will cleanse me — as I can be more like you want me to be

Being right with God in every moment is vital to our spiritual health. Not being right with God will affect the qualities leading to spiritual health we'll discuss later. Think about your life. Which is more scandalous: sinning against God or choosing to ignore that sin and God's calls for obedience?

To begin this journey well, we must start it on our knees in a spirit of confession and repentance. Will you open your heart to God today to begin this journey? Clean? Right? Eyes fixed on Jesus Christ, the Author of your faith?

Personal Reflection: *I don't like that word —
                                     ignored no*

- Can you remember a time when you despised the Word of the Lord and did evil?

- Since despising the Word of the Lord means ignoring God's commands, is there anything in your life right now that reflects despising God's Word? *I need to be reaching out to the lost.*

PRAY, visit others, show love to

- What steps can you take to live a life of awareness and obedience to the Word of the Lord?
- Reread David's prayer of repentance in Psalm 51. Use thoughts from the scripture to write a prayer of confession.

God, help me to listen to the Holy Spirit & let him to guide me to KNOW my sins that I need to repent for !!

Day Four

Walking With God

Which is easier: to say, "Your sins are forgiven,"
or to say, "Get up and walk?" Matthew 9:5

[handwritten: Not as much as I should]

Do you consistently walk with God? When we talk about walking with God, we are referring to living in God's presence and power while being obedient to His commands. What would you need for you to experience such a thing?

Are you like Peter? You heard Jesus call you to step out of the boat into the raging waves of life which frightened you. You began a walk of faith but took your eyes off Jesus and began to sink. I have good news. You know you have failed often, but God wants to walk with you. Can you think of a time when you failed God? Write about your experience.

_____

_____

_____

The Garden was a magnificent place for Adam and Eve where God met their needs and walked with them daily (Gen 3:8). I can imagine conversations they'd have as they strolled together through the garden God had prepared for them. One day, God went to meet them and called out to them, but they had hidden in the trees in shame. They had eaten the forbidden fruit, and when God questioned them, they blamed others for their disobedience. They had failed, and now instead of walking with God, they hid from Him.

We may try to hide from God in our sin, brokenness, and busyness, but we can't. After a while, we close our ears so we cannot hear His call and harden our hearts to the God who loves us. God is calling us out of our hiding places to walk with Him.

[handwritten: Do I close my ears or harden my hearts]

What's keeping you in your hiding place where you think you are hidden from God? Are you hiding for some reason and not walking with Him? Write down reasons you might hide.

I Know God Knows ever thing I do or say. I KNOW I con't hide frum God

When I walk for exercise, I begin by stretching. We should also practice a daily spiritual warmup called spiritual breathing. We ask the Holy Spirit to work in our hearts to convict us of sin, and then we agree with Him and confess our sin to God. The first step in your walk is to acknowledge the Holy Spirit who lives in you and ask by faith, "God is there any wrongdoing in my life that is keeping me from walking with You?" Have you ever asked God to work in your heart to convict you of wrongdoing? Stop for a moment and ask Him right now. *Yes more than once – Every*

Step two is to follow David's example. Read what he said in Psalm 32:5. *morning*

Psalm 32:5

"Then I acknowledged my sin to you and did not cover up my iniquity. I said, 'I will confess my transgressions to the Lord.' And you forgave the guilt of my sin."

One of the Holy Spirit's works is to convict us of sin (Jn 16:8). First John 1:9 says, "If we confess our sins, He is faithful and righteous to forgive us our sins and to cleanse us from all unrighteousness." Through confession, God lifts the weight of sin that burdens us so we can walk with Him.

Step three is to ask Him to fill us with the Holy Spirit because we want to give ourselves fully to Him. This begins the daily journey of surrender the Bible calls "walking in the Spirit" and being led by the Spirit (Gal 5:16-21). We see God's grace and mighty power at work in us and through us when we begin to walk by faith.

Years ago, after running five or six miles, I looked forward to experiencing a second wind. Without the second wind, I would have had to stop. Walking with God is about continuing to walk in the Spirit and being led by the Spirit in His power. Because of His redeeming work in us, we walk differently than before we knew Him. He empowers us and enables us to walk with Him.

He has given us a lot of help in our walk of faith. Through His Word, we have His promises, and He reminds us of the blessings He has given us so we can walk confidently with Him. Read how God reminds us through the prophet Isaiah to listen for His voice and walk in obedience.

He has also given us other believers so we can be encouraged along the way. We never walk alone because God is with us, and when we walk with God, we are

> **Isaiah 30:21**
> Whether you turn to the right or to the left, your ears will hear a voice behind you, saying, "This is the way; walk in it" (NIV).

walking with other believers on the same path. We work together, hold each other accountable, and encourage one another to walk in the way of Christ. Do you have trustworthy accountability partners? Write their names here. *Janet + Barbara / Most of my SS class*

While hiking a steep mountain in Alaska, I climbed to a ledge and entered a cleft in a rock. To my surprise, a frightened young man sat frozen in fear, and he couldn't bring himself to move forward or climb down. Fear had captured his heart. I had hiked that path before, and I knew he wasn't far from the top.

As I left to continue toward the summit, I encouraged him to keep climbing. Another friend came behind me and also encouraged the young man to continue onward. As a result of our encouragement, he followed us and made it to the top. We cheered as he made the summit.

He said, "I wouldn't have made it to the top if some friends hadn't encouraged me." As we face the challenges and opportunities of life, we have the Holy Spirit, God's Word, and other believers walking by faith with us.

John 14:6 tells us Jesus is the way. The Holy Spirit empowers us to trust God as He directs our walk. Jesus is the truth. We walk with God in His righteousness, His completeness, by His Word, and in obedience. We walk by His attributes through Christ who died for our sin and lives in us (2 Jn 1:4, Gal 5:22). He is the life. His life is empowering our lives, and in Him, we have abundant life (Jn 10:10). It is time to listen to the voice of God as He tells us, "Your sins are forgiven...get up and walk" (Mt 9:5 NIV).

Personal Reflection:

- Are you ready to live for Christ? Write a prayer expressing your intentions and ask God for His grace to help you.

- Have you counted the cost of being a disciple and what it means to walk with God? Are you ready to lay down your life for God's purposes? Write down your fears and questions about walking with God and ask Him to help you.

- Talk to another believer about walking with God. Encourage one another and pray together.

- On a scale of one to ten (ten being greatest)...
  o How is your walk with Christ?
  o Do you spend time in God's Word?
  o Are you obedient to live out the commands of Christ?
  o How is your prayer life? *should be + try more often*
  o Are you serving God by your works? *yes*
  o Are you bearing fruit in your life? *Yes*
  o Are you walking in love with others? *yes*

God if I am not doing these things
Show me where I find walking with You.
Give me your Grace to do
all of this -

Alignment With God

Have you ever cut a long piece of wood for a project? I've done repairs on several houses and often needed a piece of plywood cut down to a smaller size, like two feet by eight feet. Let's assume I don't have a chalk line. I would go to one end of the plywood and make a mark two feet from the long edge. I'd do the same on the other end and several places in between. I'd then need a straight edge to draw a line. Let's say I'm using a yardstick for my straight edge.

I've noticed when I put the straight edge on my marks, they're not in line. I'm sure it's my error in placing the mark. I know a straight line is essential. I must decide which mark to follow as a standard to make a straight line. I need at least two points. My main point of reference is my first mark closest to the edge. Next, I'll find another mark I know is two feet and use it for my second point of reference. Although I wouldn't take the time to redraw my marks, this exercise is a process to get my marks in line.

Construction work is not the only place we need alignment. We need to align our daily activities with our goals. It's important for our cars to be in good alignment, and scientists and mathematicians use alignment to decide actions concerning known formulas.

Alignment is vital to our spiritual health. We could talk about alignment with our spiritual goals or alignment with our church's purpose. Those are both important, but the main point of reference should always be alignment with God, the first mark.

> **Acts 13:22**
>
> After He had removed him (Saul), He raised up David to be their king, concerning whom He also testified and said, "I have found David the son of Jesse, a man after My heart, who will do all My will."

On Paul's first missionary journey, he stopped in Pisidian Antioch and spoke to a Jewish crowd. Read Acts 13:22 on the previous page and notice his reference to David's alignment when God chose to remove King Saul.

What is the key phrase used to describe David?

He was a man of God's will

What does that phrase mean?

God knew he asked for his
_pire to be forgiveness + ___ did God's will_

We know at least one thing a man after God's heart will do. Do you see it in the verse?

He will do God's will

Alignment with God is essential for the spiritual health of individuals and churches. As crucial as alignment is, it's often not our focus. Instead, we tend to focus on achievement instead of alignment. Do you think it's possible to experience achievement and never be aligned? What's the difference between achievement and alignment?

Ac - getting ahead
Al - Doing God's well

The first step toward aligning ourselves with God is to align our hearts with God's heart. God's focus throughout the Bible is upon our hearts. Do you remember when God told Israel, through the prophet Jeremiah, He wanted to write the law on their hearts? It wasn't just about obeying rules or jumping through religious hoops. Think about Jesus' words recorded in Matthew 22:36-38 when a lawyer asked Him for the greatest commandment.

Matthew 22:36-38

"Teacher, which is the great commandment in the Law?" 37 And He said to him, "'You shall love the Lord your God with all your heart, and with all your soul, and with all your mind.' 38 This is the great and foremost commandment."

What is Jesus saying in this command?

_____

_____

Loving God with every part of our being describes a relationship. The number one thing that will highlight and enable your alignment with God in every aspect of life is your active, growing relationship with God.

What are some qualities of a good relationship?

_____

_____

Being aligned with God's heart means we love God, but we also live according to God's commands. This truth means God's Word is essential to our daily alignment. We might consider starting our day with God in His Word as a moment of alignment. Author and podcaster, Chad Harrington said, "Spiritual disciplines are God's mechanisms for alignment."

It's important, however, as we think about spiritual disciplines, and in this case, the discipline of reading the Bible, that the focus is not upon the action of the discipline but the heart of God. God wants our hearts to be together with His as one.

If we're not careful, pride will motivate our actions and keep score of our achievements, and we'll never deepen our relationship with God. How can you read the Bible and connect to the heart of God instead of just reading to check a box?

Seek the meaning of His Word

Alignment with God's purpose is another goal as we improve our spiritual health. It's easy to focus on our purpose and ignore God's purpose altogether. If we are going to be aligned with God, one of those marks defining alignment is purpose. God's purpose.

Read Acts 13:36 on the following page. Knowing David was not always a model follower of God, how does it make you feel that Paul said King David served the purpose of God and died?

Acts 13:36

For David, after he had served the purpose of God in his own generation, fell asleep, and was laid among his fathers and underwent decay.

Wouldn't that be a great epithet to put on your tombstone? Of course, your loved ones can put it there only if it's true. What would it take for you to serve the purpose of God? What changes would you need to make in your life?

Pray, reading the Bible + seeking His meaning to it all - Allowing the Holy Spirit to guide me so I will obey God

Obeying God's commands is an essential part of serving God's purposes. The first and foremost step of obedience is surrender. Consider Philippians 2:13 "It is God who is at work in you, both to will and to work for His good pleasure."

This passage says if our hearts are willing and aligned with God's, He will work in us to accomplish His pleasure. Pause now and tell God you want to be aligned with His purpose.

The final alignment is with God's passion—the things God loves. We mess up when we love the things God does not love. Paul admonished believers in Romans 12:9 "Abhor what is evil; cling to what is good."

The Greek word for "abhor" means to have a vehement dislike for something. It's not just an aversion to something; it's a vehement dislike. Hate is an appropriate word. God tells us to hate what is evil and wrap our arms around and hold onto good things.

When we cling to what is evil and abhor what is good, we are way out of line. At the end of our lives, we will have born no fruit for God's glory.

Cars don't function well when they're out of line. Your body doesn't function well when it's out of line. Buildings can't be built, problems can't be solved, and God won't be honored without align-ment.

What will it take for you to align yourself with God? What steps will you take today?

Personal Reflection:

- Would you say you are a person after God's heart? Why or why not? Make a list of three actions you can take today to align your heart and life with God.
- Did you notice a three-letter word in Matthew 22:37 that's repeated three times? What would have to change in your life for you to love God with all your heart, soul, and mind?
- Write a prayer expressing your desire to align your life with God's heart, purposes, and passions. Tell God the steps you'll take today to begin that journey.

Lord, help me to understand what I need to change in my life to be more like Jesus —

This book

Praying

Day Six

The Power of God

Jesus replied, "You are in error because you do not know the
Scriptures or the power of God." Matthew 22:29

One of the greatest mistakes we could ever make is not to know the Scriptures or God's power. Without both the Word and God's power, we could never know salvation. In Romans 1:16, Paul says the good news is the power of God that brings salvation. God's word is "living and powerful" (Hebrews 4:12), and it is by the power of His Word all things exist and are continually sustained (Hebrews 1:3). Our salvation has become a demonstration and testimony of God's power.

It is impossible for us to imagine the power of God who brought everything into existence. His nature is eternal, and He has shared the potential of eternal life through Christ with humanity.

Consider the many aspects of His attributes. It is a great wonder God is available to us and has enabled us to know Him through His work on the cross and the resurrection. Paul says the same power that was at work in the resurrection of Christ is at work in us (Ephesians 1: 19-21). The power that animated, "God with us," is working within us and through us. His enabling power of grace makes available His blessings and empowering presence that is working through us.

Read Ephesians 1:18-21 on the following page. Paul listed several reasons why he prayed for the hearts of the Ephesians to be enlightened. Underline those reasons in the passage. How did he describe God's power? And how was God's power demonstrated?

_____

_____

_____

I remember the first time I watched a video that captured the power and terror of an atomic blast. The power and potential destruction that could come from an atom brought fear to my heart, yet I am a happy recipient of nuclear power every time I plug in a device. As believers, we know the creator of the power that is released in an atomic explosion. Even greater than an atomic explosion is the power that is at work within us to which we have access.

> **Ephesians 1:18-21**
>
> I pray that the eyes of your heart may be enlightened, so that you will know what is the hope of His calling, what are the riches of the glory of His inheritance in the saints, [19] and what is the surpassing greatness of His power toward us who believe. These are in accordance with the working of the strength of His might [20] which He brought about in Christ, when He raised Him from the dead and seated Him at His right hand in the heavenly places, [21] far above all rule and authority and power and dominion, and every name that is named, not only in this age but also in the one to come.

God's power is working in our hearts. We cannot see the spiritual things without help, just like we cannot see atoms without a powerful microscope. Without God's Spirit and His Word, we cannot see Him working. When God moves in our spirits for His purposes, He brings about change in our world. God wants to change our world from inside out through His power and presence within us.

Most of us would say it would be difficult to live without electrical power, yet when it comes to spiritual things, we don't stay plugged in to Christ by remaining in Him. We remain in Christ through the working of God's grace, by walking in His Spirit, and through obedience to His commands (Jn 15:10). We are obedient because we love Him (Jn 14:23). Sin will destroy this unity we can have in Christ, and without Him we could accomplish nothing with eternal value (Jn 15:5). The power of man accomplishes something in the short term but not with eternal consequences. How have you experienced the oneness of being in Christ? Have you experienced that same unity among your brothers and sisters in Christ?

Jesus tells us faith the size of a mustard seed can move mountains, and nothing is impossible for those who have such faith (Mt17:20). Knowing the working power of God that comes by faith and that we have direct access to God's power, we experience both confidence and competence concerning the work that is to be accomplished in Jesus' name (2 Cor 3:4,5). Even Jesus could do very little in His hometown because of the people's lack of faith and belief (Lk 5:16-30). How many sick could have been healed and marriages restored? How many could have been delivered from demonic forces and known forgiveness of sin? But they did not recognize Jesus as their Messiah. As God's people, we live by faith, and by faith nothing is impossible.

How do we have access to God's power, and how do we serve God in His power and strength? We continue to follow Christ in the same way we first met Him and experienced His working power in our hearts. It is by grace through faith that God works in us and through us. The working of His power is always in agreement with His will. How do we know His will? We know it through His Word and by His Spirit leading and guiding us.

We cannot become a healthy church until we become spiritually healthy individuals in whom God works by demonstrating His mighty power. I alone am not a healthy church, nor am I the church. At the same time, the church cannot be spiritually healthy unless I am spiritually healthy

The Bible tells us in the final days there will be "terrible times," and there will be individuals who have "a form of godliness but deny its power." Paul warns Timothy to "have nothing to do with those people" (2 Tim 3:1-5 NIV). We see this very thing happening today. Nothing can be accomplished without Christ working through His people by grace through faith. Anyone who denies the power of

God will not experience the work of God, and those around them will suffer. Have we not been recipients of God's grace? What are we missing because of our lack of faith?

Personal Reflection

- In what areas of your life are you not trusting God and not believing in the working of His grace and power?
- The Bible teaches we must remain in Christ by loving Him and by obeying His commands. In what areas are you being disobedient?
- What steps can you take to help you walk in Christ so He can work in you and through you?
- Sometimes, we are quick to judge others for lacking faith, but how can you humbly encourage other believers to have faith so God can work through His people (the Church)?

When I pray & pray for God to stop the shooting, killing, etc. I know He can do it — He had the singers fall into the earth — why cant He do that now. What can I do to see changes needed in my "world"

To stop wars

The Provision of God

God said to Moses, "I Am who I Am;" and He said, "Thus you
shall say to the sons of Israel, I Am has sent me to you." Exodus 3:14

I approached the sandy beach on Lake O' the Pines and stared at the lonely sailboat. I'd never sailed before, but how hard could it be? I pushed out onto the water to take my maiden voyage, the wind blowing through my hair and filling up the sail.

All went well for a while as the boat picked up speed. The wind drove me across the calm water, and I felt like a bird gliding through the air—until the wind stopped. And so did my boat. I gained a new appreciation for being "dead in the water." After waiting to no avail for the wind to return, I slipped into the water and swam for shore while pulling the boat behind me.

I noticed three kinds of boats that day: canoes, motorboats, and sailboats. Motorboats are run on gasoline and canoes by human energy, but sailboats are propelled by the wind.

When we consider spiritual health, we must ask ourselves what's running our lives? What is providing the necessary energy for us to grow, flourish, and bear fruit for God's glory? It's not a what but a who. God must be the energy that fills our sails, and when God fills our sails, the wind never stops.

The Bible reminds us in 2 Peter 1:3, "By his divine power, God has given us everything we need for living a godly life" (NLT). Do you believe that verse? Yes

God's provision begins with our salvation. We don't add anything to the equation that makes our eternal salvation possible. Read Titus 3:5-7. What is the basis of salvation?

God's mercy — His grace

So many words in that passage are powerful, but one of them is *richly*. Without holding back, God poured his mercy on us richly and with abundance. You don't deserve His mercy, and you can't earn it. You can only receive it.

Titus 3:5-7

He saved us, not on the basis of deeds which we have done in righteousness, but according to His mercy, by the washing of regeneration and renewing by the Holy Spirit, 6 whom He poured out upon us richly through Jesus Christ our Savior, 7 so that being justified by His grace we would be made heirs according to *the* hope of eternal life.

God has also provided everything you need to fulfill your calling and honor Him. Look at the opening scripture from Exodus 3:14. Why did God choose "I Am" for His name?

_____

_____

We can connect the meaning of the name, "I Am," to the God Who is always present, and we can also see it as the God Who always provides. Moses struggled with his calling to go before Pharoah. He didn't think he was capable of such a mission. Do you believe God calls us only on missions we can do in our strength? Have you ever felt incapable of doing something you thought God was calling you to do? Write a few thoughts about that experience.

Yes, but after praying I could do it. I still struggle to tell people about Jesus

Henry Blackaby wrote, "Some people say, 'God will never ask me to do something I can't do.' I've come to the place in my life that if the assignment I sense God giving me is something I know I can handle, I know it's probably not from God. The kind of assignments God gives in the Bible is always God-sized."[1] God's assignments are God-sized because He wants to reveal Himself to the world through us.

Moses said he couldn't take the assignment because he couldn't speak well. Some thought he may have had a speech impediment.

Do you think a speech impediment will stop the voice of God or hinder His plans? God used a shepherd boy with a sling to kill a giant. He used a poor Jewish girl (Esther) to save Jewish exiles. He used a little boy with five loaves and two fish to feed thousands of people.

The Bible says God is Jehovah Jireh, our Provider. God isn't looking for ability; He's looking for obedience. God doesn't need what you have. He just wants to involve you in His plans. Isn't that truth amazing? The God of the universe wants to include you in His eternal work on Earth. Even God's call is an act of grace, an expression of His abundant mercy poured without measure upon us.

> **2 Corinthians 9:8**
>
> "And God is able to make all grace abound to you, so that always having all sufficiency in everything, you may have an abundance for every good deed."

Read 2 Corinthians 9:8. Do you believe God can make all grace abound to you? What is the result of this abundant provision?

Yes — I can do what He wants me to do —

God not only provides for every good deed but also provides for every need. God said He provides every need according to His riches in glory (Phil 4:19). He provides a way of escape when we are tempted to sin (1 Cor 10:13), strength for the weary when we feel we could go no further (Isa 40:29), and a path through the wilderness when there seems to be no way out (Isa 43:19). God is our Provider.

You may say, "I need money, buildings, or material things!" What does Matthew 6:26 say about God's provision?

> **Matthew 6:26**
>
> "Look at the birds of the air, that they do not sow, nor reap nor gather into barns, and *yet* your heavenly Father feeds them. Are you not worth much more than they?"

_____

_____

_____

God knows your needs. Imagine a wealthy and righteous ruler with a son who will soon lead the kingdom. Isn't the material wealth of the ruler also available to his son? We are God's children, and Jesus has all we need. We have a heavenly Father who cares for us.

When I was stuck on Lake O' the Pines years ago, boats weren't the only things on the lake. I was. In a sense, that lake has become a picture of my life. Looking back, I realize I have three choices for how I will live by faith and serve God. I can be like a motorboat and depend on some outside source for fuel, but external sources are limited. I can be like a canoe, but I know I don't have the power to live the Christian life by my means. Or I can be like a sailboat. The good news is God wants to fill my sails with a continuous flow of His Spirit. The only way I can live a godly life, bear eternal fruit, and enjoy the abundance for which God made me is to hoist my sails high and be driven through life on the wind and power and provision of Almighty God.

Personal Reflection:

- Have you ever tried to work in your strength rather than depending upon the provision of God? Describe the situation below. *Yes! Yes! Yes!*

- Is God calling you to a God-sized task? Do you realize He'll provide all you need to accomplish it? What might keep you from being obedient?

- Write a prayer expressing gratitude for God's provision and surrender to His Spirit.

I need to pray, Lord, ~~before~~ I act! I need to listen to the Holy Spirit + turn it all to God!

Day Eight

Our Dependence Upon God

So it came about when Moses held his hand up, that Israel
prevailed, and when he let his hand down, Amalek prevailed.
12 But Moses' hands were heavy. Then they took a stone
and put it under him, and he sat on it; and Aaron and Hur
supported his hands, one on one side and one on the other.
Thus his hands were steady until the sun set. Exodus 17:11-12

Everyone lives by rules, regulations, or structures. Everything
exists within a framework that governs order and purpose. One of
the first ways I learned to share my faith was with *The Four Spiritual*
Laws written by Bill Bright. It begins by saying, "Just as there are
physical laws that govern the universe, so are there spiritual laws
that govern your relationship with God."

We were created to be in a relationship with God, and without
Him, we wouldn't have life or eternity. Jesus said the quality of
things He provides for us is greater than anything the world can
give. He tells us there is a peace the
world gives, and there is the peace
God gives, and the two are not the
same (John 14:22). God is love (1 Jn
4:8), and Jesus is our peace (Eph
2:14).

> **James 1:17**
>
> "Every good thing given
> and every perfect gift is
> from above, coming down
> from the Father of lights,
> with whom there is no
> variation or shifting sha-
> dow."

The essence of God, His attributes and character, are present
within us, and we are dependent
upon God to work through us.
James wrote about one aspect of God's character in James 1:17.
How does he refer to God, and how does he describe God's gifts?

_____

The question becomes, "Who will I depend upon?" You may say, "I will depend upon no one," but that will never be true. We are more dependent upon systems and individuals than ever before.

But what about God? Do you depend upon Him? How? When?

I depend on Him to keep me on the right path & to obey Him

All creation expresses dependence. The Scripture says Christ, the Creator, holds all things together (Col 1:17).

Our physical bodies are dependent on many parts working together so we can live and function. When something goes wrong, doctors discover the problem and help the body heal. We are even dependent upon bacteria existing inside our bodies to help us function properly. God created the body to function as it does, and He knew us before we were in the womb (Jer. 1:5). We are dependent!

The Body of Christ, His Church, is an organism of many functioning parts. We are not able to operate effectively as individuals without the Holy Spirit. Without the empowered Body of Christ working as one, we cannot fulfill God's purpose. There are no "by myself" churches.

Jesus said believers are dependent on the vine to be fruitful. The Bible teaches this truth, and creation shouts, "You serve a God of abundance who created you to be abundantly fruitful." Without dependence on Jesus, we are fruitless, ineffective, disobedient, unable to live abundant lives, and unable to please God (John 10:10).

Why do we scream independence and try to take lordship for ourselves? Why do we become so self-centered, arrogant, and rebellious? Why do we deny God and His power by trying to do the work ourselves instead of going to the Lord and asking what He wants us to do? _Pride –_

We often start planning and then ask for God's blessings. We are self-oriented because of our sinful nature that began with our rebellion against God in the Garden. Selfishness was Satan's

Satan

motivation, and to this day, he works to destroy God's creation and God's people.

Think of a time you tried to work independently from God. _Yes._ Have you ever planned and asked God for His blessing later? If so, write about your experience. Ask God what you should do differently in the future.

Sometimes it went well + some time it was a failure~ PRIDE!

We must humble ourselves to find success that comes through dependence upon God. When we are humble before God, we become spiritually healthy, fruitful, and one with Christ and His Church. Through humility, we are lifted from our failures (James 4:10). Are you humble? How would humility change your life toward God and others?

Working on it hardly

We see our dependence upon God, individually and corporately, in the story of Moses referenced above. In this Bible story, soldiers were battling, giving their all to obtain a victory, but they were dependent upon Moses lifting his arms to the throne of God, who brings victory. The Amalekites were the enemy who raised their hands against God's throne (Ex 17:16).

Moses was the leader of the people, and his arms grew tired and frail. If he didn't lift his arms, his army would lose the battle. Aaron and Hur, faithful friends who stood beside Moses, held up his arms until Israel won the battle. God, whose power worked to help the soldiers overcome the enemy of Israel, was the crucial figure in this story. God could have destroyed the Amalekites with a simple word, but He chose another way that called for dependence upon Him.

We do not have the power to win battles without God or one another. He has invited us to join Him in His work, but He must lead. It is impossible to fight our spiritual battles, grow in our faith,

find unity with God and one another, or fulfill God's purposes without Him. We are dependent upon God and all He has promised.

Personal Reflection:

- How do you express your dependence upon God for victory in life?

- Do you depend upon God for abundance when you serve in your church?   *I hope so*

- Are you holding up someone's arms? Write down their names and pray for them now.   *I try —*

- Do you have people like Moses who lift their arms for you? Thank God for them and pray for them.   *Many & I do pray for them*

- Do you know anyone fighting spiritual battles who needs some-one to hold up their arms? Pray for them now and send them a note of encouragement.   *?*

- If you have experienced a victory, share it, and celebrate God's work by giving thanks to Him.

Scripture Memory Verse
Philippians 3:10-11 that I may know Him and the power of His resurrection and the fellowship of His sufferings, being conformed to His death; [11] in order that I may attain to the resurrection from the dead

Growth Forces

I've always been puzzled by the children's nursery rhyme: "Mary, Mary quite contrary, how does your garden grow..." I'm puzzled because being contrary is a negative trait, or is it? I thought the word meant to be disagreeable. That's true, but it also means doing the opposite of what is expected or desired. So, I suppose being contrary is not necessarily negative. The rhyme says Mary worked her garden an opposite way from what someone expected.

If silver bells and cockleshells and pretty maids in a row aren't the expected fruit of a garden, what is? That's a great question, and we'll consider the answer in this next section. For the next six days, we'll focus on six different growth forces suggested by Christian Schwarz in his book, *Color Your World with Natural Church Development*.

What do you suppose he meant by a growth force? We understand growth from a spiritual perspective. We want to grow to be more Christlike and want our character to reflect the nature of Christ. We want to mature in our faith and our knowledge of the Word of God. The question is, what will cause this maturity to happen?

The concept of growth forces points to the existence of a force or power that creates the natural byproduct of growth. Notice I used the word natural. It's natural because the byproduct, or fruit, of our spiritual garden happens by itself if the environment is right.

Consider life as a garden. When you plant vegetables in a garden, you don't focus on the vegetables; you focus on the proper environment that will cause vegetables to flourish. If you pull the weeds, make sure the right nutrients are in the soil, ensure your garden gets enough water and sunlight, and keep the pests from destroying your garden, the fruit will naturally grow.

Growth forces point to energy or spiritual resources that work together to produce spiritual fruit. You can look at each of the six forces independently, but you must also see they have to work together to produce the most significant spiritual health in an individual and a church.

As you move through the next six days, consider the growth force that is the focus of the day, but also know it is working in conjunction with other forces in your life (we mention six in this section). Think about how God uses these forces to produce spiritual health and how Christians work together to experience a synergistic benefit, ultimately producing unimaginable fruit.

It's our prayer as you spend time thinking about and praying through these forces, you will look for barriers that have been hindering the release of these forces in your life. We hope you will find these growth forces a natural byproduct of walking with God's Spirit and experiencing the power needed to develop the qualities required for great spiritual fruit. In John 15:8, Jesus said, "My Father is glorified by this, that you bear much fruit, and so prove to be My disciples."

Day Nine

Interdependence

We are to grow up in all aspects into Him who is the head, even Christ, [16] *from whom the whole body, being fitted and held together by what every joint supplies, according to the proper working of each individual part, causes the growth of the body for the building up of itself in love.*
Ephesians 4:15-16

My wife and I have six children, and as parents, we want our children to mature and serve the Lord. We're at the stage where they are all adults. Our fifth child graduated from college last week, and our youngest turns twenty-one this year. It's been a blessing to watch them grow and pursue their passions. Our goals for them have been spiritual maturity, physical wholeness, and emotional well-being. God has these same goals for His children.

One significant mark of maturity is interdependence, the first growth force for life and spiritual health. The Bible mentions this force in various ways, and the principle impacts almost every area of life.

The first two stages of maturity and well-being are easy to achieve. The first, dependence, comes naturally at birth. We all understand what it means to need someone. We previously looked at our dependence upon God, and we can also relate to our dependence upon others.

Our parents work to help us find independence through the early years. We learn to feed ourselves, tie our shoes, and wake up with an alarm clock. Independence is essential, but if we stop there, we'll miss out on greater levels of fruitfulness.

Interdependence is the level of existence when we learn to rely upon one another to fulfill our needs and accomplish our purposes. Interdependence is a higher level because it requires humility and sacrifice. It involves looking for ways to contribute to the well-being of others while benefiting from their contributions.

When Paul wrote to the church at Ephesus, he challenged them to grow in the Lord. The fourth chapter of Ephesians calls the church to maturity and unity and leads Christians to focus on their interconnectedness with other believers.

The passage above says we are "fitted and held together by what every joint supplies." You supply something to the function of your relationships within the Body of Christ. This passage calls you a "joint." In the grand picture of the Church as a body, you may be a knuckle, an elbow, or a kneecap, but you have an essential part to play in the function of the whole.

Before God made Eve, He revealed Adam was incomplete by himself. Read Genesis 2:18. Why was it not good for man to be alone?

It's Not good for anyone to be alone

Genesis 2:18

Whenever God said Eve would be *suitable* for him, He was saying she'd fill gaps in Adam's life. Did God make a mistake by making Adam with gaps? Of course not.

Then the Lord God said, "It is not good for the man to be alone; I will make him a helper suitable for him."

God gave Adam gaps on purpose because He wanted him to work interdependently with someone He would provide.

The focus of Ephesians 4:15-16 is when each part of the Body of Christ functions properly, the rest of the Body benefits. The result of such interdependence is the growth of the Church and the consequence of love.

I'm sure you remember John Dunne's famous poem: "No man is an island, entire of itself; every man is a piece of the continent, a part of the main." We're an essential part of the whole.

The principle of interdependence is not just about relationships with other people. Interdependence also points to individual parts or aspects of our lives working together to achieve spiritual health and fruitfulness. As long as we don't restrict this process, interdependence will happen automatically as various healthy qualities and aspects work together for a more significant benefit.

We will look at eight quality characteristics later in our study, and you'll discover each quality works interdependently to strengthen your spiritual life. If you become aware of this process, you can lean into it and glean the positive outcome of this combined function of the different qualities.

For example, loving relationships will be critical to a healthy gift-based ministry. If we're not walking with Christ and loving one another, the ministry effectiveness of individual Christians and the Church will be diminished.

Can you see how passionate spirituality will support inspiring worship? The deeper you grow in your relationship with Jesus (passionate spirituality), the greater will be your expressions of private and public worship (inspiring worship).

To grasp the growth force of interdependence fully, you need to consider using one quality characteristic that may be a strength to shore up areas of greater weakness. As you work through the eight characteristics, try to determine which may be your "minimum factor" as an individual follower of Jesus.

If you're going through the evaluation process as a church, you'll be looking at your church's minimum factor, but don't miss out on the opportunity to find an area in your personal life to develop. If you're not using Natural Church Development to evaluate your church, you can use these principles personally to grow in your spiritual life.

Suppose effective structures are your strongest area and passionate spirituality is your weakest. How can you use the strength of effective structures to help build your spiritual life?

Interdependence is a natural part of life because God built it into your life system. Many people never touch this critical area that leads to significant personal growth. I hope you'll think collectively about your relationships and the qualities that lead to spiritual health. Allow those areas to work together to take you to greater heights in your spiritual life.

Personal Reflection:
- How have you experienced interdependence in relationships with other Christians?
- Are you part of a ministry team in your church? How do the gifts of those team members support one another?
- Consider your spiritual health. Can you think of several factors that work together to lead to greater health?
- Write a prayer asking God to show you how to use the strong areas of your life and faith to strengthen the weaker areas. Also, tell God you want to work interdependently with others to accomplish His purposes and strengthen the Body of Christ.

*5. 5.

*Dod's Girls   +

Showers

Meals for funerals

Lord help me to work to
glorify You & to help others
Help me to not be Work for other
                    to see me

for me

Day Ten

Multiplication

God blessed them; and God said to them,
"Be fruitful and multiply..." Genesis 1:28

What is God's first command? God told Adam and Eve to have babies. Multiply! God made us to have children. Dan and I have tried to do our part. I have six children, and he has five—plus many grandchildren!

I'm not writing today's devotional to address whether we should have children but to talk about the natural growth force of multiplication. It's natural because you see it in every area of nature—trees birth new trees, birds birth new birds, and fish birth new fish.

From a spiritual point of view, what does multiplication mean for the Christian?

When God used the word "multiply" in His first command, it had significant meaning. He didn't tell the first couple to add to the earth. Christian Schwarz, founder of Natural Church Development, teaches addition is the opposite of multiplication in church development. My wife and I added six children to the population, but the multiplication process begins when they have children.

If each of my children has six children, Christmas get-togethers will be crazy and thrilling.

I ask the question again, "What does multiplication mean for you?" Like worship, tithing, and prayer, multiplication is a part of your Christian experiences, but what are you supposed to multiply, and what does multiplication mean in the context of spiritual health?

Christian Schwarz said, "Multiplication...means striving to give birth to new organisms, that themselves will give birth to new organisms." We know God's first command for Adam and Eve was for physical multiplication but read Matthew 28:19-20 to see another type of multiplication.

One aspect of multiplication is making disciples. It's more than just making converts; that's addition. Multiplication happens when we make multiplying converts who are not only leading others to Jesus but are also bearing fruit.

> **Matthew 28:19-20**
>
> "Go therefore and make disciples of all the nations, baptizing them in the name of the Father and the Son and the Holy Spirit, 20 teaching them to observe all that I commanded you; and lo, I am with you always, even to the end of the age."

Have you ever led someone to faith in Christ? Sharing Jesus makes a lot of people nervous. Why do you think some Christians are afraid to be a witness?

Afraid of what to say
" of them Not
~~Listen them~~ them
reject

Satan must love it when we are fearful of talking about the most crucial topic in the world. How can we overcome our fear? Knowing what to say is helpful. You can study the "How to Become a Christian" portion at the back of this book to learn how to lead someone to faith in Jesus. I have people tell me they're afraid someone will ask them a question they can't answer.

We base this fear upon the belief we are supposed to know all the answers. Only Jesus knows all the answers. If you share your faith with someone and he asks you a question you can't answer, you can say, "I don't know the answer to that, but I'll try to find it. What I do know is Jesus died so my sin can be forgiven, and I have a new life in Him." Pick up with where you were sharing the gospel before the question.

Multiplying is more than making converts to Christianity. If you lead one person to Jesus every day for a year, you have 365 new Christians. In five years, you have 1,825 new believers. In ten years, there are 3,650 new people in the family of God. Awesome!

What if you led one person to Jesus every six months, but you helped them grow in their faith, bear Kingdom fruit, and taught them how to be a witness during the six months? So, at the end of six months, both of you would lead one more person to faith in Christ. At the end of one year, there'd be you and three new multiplying disciples. Do you know how many growing, multiplying disciples you'd have in ten years from one faithful person leading one person to Jesus every six months and helping them to become multiplying disciples in the same way? 1,048,576! Compare the two models: 3,650 converts from addition type evangelism versus 1,048,576 new growing, multiplying believers from a multiplication type of discipleship. Do you know what you'd have from that model after twenty years? Take a guess. Here's a clue. You'd reach the entire state of California in year thirteen. You'd run out of people to reach in seventeen years because you'd reach the world's entire population. Is it any wonder Jesus told us to make disciples instead of converts?

What challenges are keeping you from applying the multiplication principle to evangelism and making disciples? How can you overcome these challenges?

Holy Spirit,
God will tell you
what to say. Trust
them

2 Timothy 2:1-3

You therefore, my son, be strong in the grace that is in Christ Jesus. ² The things which you have heard from me in the presence of many witnesses, entrust these to faithful men who will be able to teach others also. ³ Suffer hardship with *me,* as a good soldier of Christ Jesus.

We also can't think of multiplication as just an evangelistic strategy. It has to be a lifestyle incorporated into every aspect of our lives. One of our goals is to multiply spiritual fruit, Christlikeness, faith, and obedience in other people.

Read 2 Timothy 2:1-3 and consider critical principles connected to the growth force of multiplication.

You will notice a few themes found within the principle of multiplication. One is relationship. How did Paul refer to Timothy? (_my_   _son_)

Paul mentored young Timothy in his faith. Timothy had significant spiritual influence from his mother and grandmother, but Paul stepped in and helped the young man walk to a new place on his spiritual journey.

Are you helping anyone on that journey? If not, who can you mentor spiritually?

_____

Can you see the multiplication factor where Paul nurtured his young friend, Timothy, and challenged him to find other men he would encourage? Not only is the process of multiplication relational, but it's also intentional. Paul told Timothy to find someone faithful who would continue the multiplication process.

Think about how you multiply Christ's character through others. Consider your role in multiplying through your children, your friends, small group members, and believers at church. In what other areas of life can you multiply the gospel, Christ's character, and Kingdom fruit?

_____

_____

Personal Reflection:
- How have you seen the principle of multiplication at work in your life? Think beyond the ordinary concepts, such as children and sharing the gospel.
- Have you ever led anyone to Jesus? *Yes but not many* How would you share the gospel differently in response to the multiplication principle?
- Think of other areas in your life that call for the multiplication principle. Make a list. How can you multiply Christ's character, spiritual fruit, and Kingdom life through others? Through whom can you multiply these truths today?
- Write a prayer expressing your desire to God to multiply His character, share the gospel through multiplication, and bear Kingdom fruit in yourself and through others.

Day Eleven

Energy Transformation

For this purpose also I labor, striving according to His power,
which mightily works within me. Colossians 1:29

Lab—in s ca Labs

When was the last time you changed energy from one form to another? Have you eaten today? Eating is transforming chemical energy into mechanical energy to enable your body to function. If you're sitting in the comfort of a climate-controlled building, your comfort is the product of electrical energy transformed into kinetic energy. We benefit from multiple energy transformations daily.

Walking in the Spirit is another form of energy transformation. Reread Colossians 1:29 at the top of today's study. In verse twenty-eight of that chapter, Paul states his goal is to present everyone as a mature believer. Then, he makes the powerful statement of the verse above. What two words did he use to describe his effort?

He labors - using God's power

Are "labor" and "striving" the same thing? The word translated as labor means to work hard like we should do most of the time. We work to accomplish a task. Labor can describe the general task of working, but it points to the fact the worker is "all in."

"Striving" means straining. It's saying that Paul is using every ounce of his strength and effort to accomplish this vital goal. As important as it is to work and strain toward a goal, our plans aren't big enough if our spiritual goals can be accomplished through our efforts. Kingdom goals require energy that's not our own.

Look at the following four words from Colossians 1:29: "according to His power." Whose power is working in Paul to accomplish this goal? You got it. God's power works in us to achieve Kingdom goals.

Have you ever tackled a job you knew was Kingdom work and would require God's power to work through you? Make a note that will remind you of that circumstance.

Teaching S.S & letting Holy Spirit help me -
VBS

When you finished the task, could you sense your accomplishment happened because of God's energy at work in your life? I sense that often when I write or preach. It's humbling to know you are being used as a conduit for God's power, and His power is available for all of us.

This example is an exciting illustration of energy transformation, but the principle can be seen in other areas of our lives. Sports teams take advantage of energy transformation all the time. For example, they pull energy from the hype of a rivalry game and transfer the energy to effort on the field. We may call it momentum.

As believers, we can draw energy from one another or our circumstances. I've used the energy of good news to help me stay up a little longer when writing a book. Can you think of biblical examples of energy transformation where power was taken from one thing, circumstance, or person and used in another?

The Israelites used energy transfer all the time. Throughout the Old Testament days, Jewish people were an aural society and often told stories of God working in the past to inspire faith for the future. God told Joshua to pull twelve stones from the Jordan River to remind future generations of how God had delivered Israel—energy transformation. Do you suppose those stones encouraged future generations to trust in the Lord?

Have you ever drawn energy from one area (thing, person, event, etc.) and used it in another? Write a few words of explanation and share them with a friend.

Energy from S. S, members — that I
rely on -
Barbara praying for me

When we look at the quality characteristics in the final section of this study, look for ways you can transfer energy from one strong characteristic to bolster an area that's not so strong. For example, if you are strong in creating systems or utilizing structures to accomplish goals and your life and find energy in doing so, how can you use that energy to strengthen a weaker area? If passionate spirituality is a weaker area, use the energy gleaned from planning and organizing and create a plan or system to grow deeper in your relationship with Christ. If loving relationships aren't so strong, use the energy you gain from putting together effective structures to create a system that will help you communicate love to others in a better way.

Energy transformation doesn't always come from favorable circumstances. You can draw energy from something terrible and turn it into something good.

I recently followed Tiger Woods' return to professional golf when he entered the Master's Golf Tournament in Augusta, Georgia. You may know Tiger was in a car accident almost two years ago that could have killed him. Some said he'd never walk again. Everyone seemed stunned he would give it a try at the most prestigious tournament in the golf world.

Only fifty golfers advanced to the final two days of play, and Tiger had the opportunity to advance. At the end of the tournament, he finished forty-seventh. It will probably go down as one of the worst finishes of his professional career, but he smiled throughout his interview afterward.

I have a theory. Tiger Woods had to know he wouldn't play well, but he attempted it anyway. I think he wanted to create an energy transformation experience from a failed Master's attempt for his comeback. Considering his injuries, just the fact that he finished was a huge accomplishment, but his poor score will motivate him to get up every day and go through the paces of getting back into top shape.

Have you ever used a negative experience to build positive energy? Write a few words about that experience.

_____

_____

Can you think of biblical examples of something terrible being used to promote something good?

_____ _Easter in bondage — she was able to_ _____

Safe her people —

_____

_____

The story of Joseph comes to mind. Do you remember when Joseph, once a slave and prisoner, now second in command to Pharaoh, confronts his brothers? Read the verse in the box that relates part of that confrontation.

> **Genesis 50:19-20**
>
> But Joseph said to them, "Do not be afraid, for am I in God's place? 20 As for you, you meant evil against me, *but* God meant it for good in order to bring about this present result, to preserve many people alive."

Christian persecution in the New Testament is another biblical example. God used the persecution of believers (bad) to spread the gospel around the world (good). The early Christian author Tertullian said, "The blood of the martyrs is the seed of the church." Romans 8:28 reminds us, "And we know that God causes all things to work together for good to those who love God, to those who are called according to *His* purpose."

Turning negative energy, or even positive energy, into something good is not just positive thinking. It requires faith that God will use everything in our lives for good if we let Him. It's also faith to know if something passed through the hands of our Heavenly Father and entered our lives, we must view it as a good gift, even if it's painful. God is in the redeeming business, and He will redeem all things in our lives for His purposes.

Energy transformation also requires thought. Think about the energy found in the people, circumstances, and events of your life. How can you allow God to transform the energy into Kingdom fruit for your good and His glory?

Personal Reflection:

- Walking in the Spirit means living our lives in step with God's will and purpose while drawing from His presence and power. This type of energy transformation requires surrender, obedience, and faith. What choices can you make this week to walk in God's Spirit? *Pray more — Give God the glory*

- Create a plan to describe how you will use energy transformation in your life to accomplish God's goals for you.

- Write a prayer expressing thanks to God for His power that works mightily in you (Colossians 1:29 declares it is God's energy that energizes us). Express to God your willingness to use good and bad situations to find the energy to follow His plan for your life.

Lord, help me draw on Your power — but let me give You all the glory!

Sustainability

For I am confident of this very thing, that He who began a good work in you will perfect it until the day of Christ Jesus. Philippians 1:6

I ran cross-country in college and learned an important lesson about sustainability. Competing teams often used a "jackrabbit" to get us to run a pace that wasn't sustainable throughout the race. If this opposing runner could start the race at a sprint, my team was tempted to sprint after him. If we did so, the other team would run their normal race speed and pass us when we were exhausted. We learned to ignore the jackrabbit and make sure our pace was something we could sustain the entire race.

Sustainability is a vital growth force that leads us to new heights of spiritual health and enables us to pass on health to the next generation. We must learn we don't generate spiritual sustainability; God does.

Notice the opening verse above says, "He who began a good work." Of course, "He" is Jesus. God is the One who started the work of salvation in us and will continue throughout our lives. Think of salvation in three aspects or phases: justification, sanctification, and glorification.

We don't use those theological terms often, but they are essential to our faith journey. Being justified means being forgiven or made just. Justification happens the moment we surrender to Jesus and become Christians. Sanctification is the process of being made holy or set apart, and this process occurs throughout our Christian life. Salvation is not only an act but also a process. That's why Paul could say Jesus is perfecting God's good work in us until the day of Christ Jesus.

The final stage is glorification. This last step of salvation happens when God takes us out of this world to the next. We will have new bodies and a life that never ends.

Someone defined these stages as the three tenses of salvation. We were saved from the penalty of sin (justification), we are being saved from the power of sin (sanctification), and we will be saved from the presence of sin (glorification).

Notice in all three stages God is the one doing the work. Spiritual health is sustainable because God is working in our lives.

> **Galatians 5:16-18**
>
> But I say, walk by the Spirit, and you will not carry out the desire of the flesh. 17 For the flesh sets its desire against the Spirit, and the Spirit against the flesh; for these are in opposition to one another, so that you may not do the things that you please. 18 But if you are led by the Spirit, you are not under the Law.

In Galatians 5, God inspired Paul to admonish believers to live in the spiritual freedom God offers through redemption. He urged us to serve, not "devour," one another with hateful attitudes. Read Galatians 5:16-18. How does Paul say we are to overcome the desire of the flesh? _Walk with the Spirit_

What did he mean by "walk by the Spirit"? _We will do God's will— Not ours_

God tells us His Spirit comes to live within us when we become followers of Jesus (Acts 2:38, Rom. 8:9). Ephesians 5:18 commands us to continue to be filled with the Spirit. I once read Warren Wiersbe taught being filled with the Spirit is not getting more of God's Spirit but allowing the Spirit to have more of us.

Galatians 5:18 speaks of another aspect of walking by the Spirit. What word did God use? _We live in God's power_

Walking by the Spirit and being led by the Spirit are synonymous concepts. When we walk by the Spirit, we live daily in God's power and enjoy the reality of His presence. We overcome sin by either recognizing temptation and standing firm in obedience or by seeing instantly we have disobeyed God. We confess our sin and step back into fellowship with Christ.

God wants us to overcome sin for many reasons, but one is it hinders spiritual sustainability. Satan is a destroyer, and he wants to rob us of spiritual fruit. We sustain spiritual health so we can pass spiritual fruit to the next generation.

How does an apple tree sustain life for future apple trees? It's through the seed in the fruit. Our spiritual fruit also provides the seed of sustainability as it impacts others with the message of the gospel and the call to live in God's Spirit.

We know through studies that children of abusers become abusers. In the same vein, we also know that children of spiritually healthy believers become spiritually healthy believers. The spiritual fruit is passed on to future generations.

Consider the contrast between two colonial families. We know the first as the Jukes clan. Jukes may not have been their real name because Mr. Jukes changed his name numerous times to avoid arrest. He was shiftless and lazy. The local sheriff arrested him many times, but he continued to get into trouble. His wife was a drunkard, so I can imagine the sad shape of their household.

Of his 1200 descendants, at least 400 were drunkards or drug addicts, 300 were professional beggars, and more than a hundred were convicted criminals. Seven were convicted murderers, and more than fifty spent time in mental institutions.

Following in his father's and grandfather's footsteps, a contemporary of Mr. Jukes, Jonathan Edwards, became a preacher. Some say he was one of the greatest theologians and philosophers from America. God used his preaching to spark a tremendous spiritual awakening, and he became the third president of Princeton.

The Edwards family had 400 descendants. One was the vice-president of the United States, three were U.S. senators, three were governors, thirteen served as college and university presidents, and thirty were judges. Sixty-five worked as college professors, and 100 were ministers, missionaries, or seminary professors. Another 100 were lawyers, and sixty were doctors. Several wrote books and published newspapers.

Spiritual health is sustainable through the fruit in our lives and by the work of God's Spirit. What is the key to sustainability? It's God in us. Following Jesus calls for daily surrender, and as we submit to God's authority, spiritual fruit is born in us that blesses our lives and spills over into future generations.

I have humbled myself

Personal Reflection:

- Has God begun a good work in you? How have you seen Him work in your life since you became a follower of Jesus?

- What steps can you take to walk in God's Spirit? Are those steps different than how you're living now? What changes are needed to sustain spiritual health and pass it to the next generation?

- Write a prayer expressing your desire to sustain spiritual health throughout your life. Ask God to give you insight into bearing fruit and impacting the next generation.

Lord help me change to sustain spiritual health & help me to pass it on to the next generation —

Mutually Beneficial Relationships

I was just a kid the first time I saw a shark when I went snorkeling. It was small, so I suppose it would have had to gnaw me to death if it wanted to eat me. I would have swum for the boat, except I didn't have one; we were snorkeling from the beach.

One thing caught my attention, something I've noticed each time I've seen a shark while diving: the shark had a little fish attached to it. On that day in Panama City Beach, this small shark had only one. I've seen bigger sharks with multiple little suckerfish attached. These miniature scavengers are called "remoras." They enjoy a mutually beneficial, or as scientists would say, symbiotic relationship with the giant shark.

Remoras attach to sharks or other large sea creatures and eat the parasites that would cause harm to the shark. These little hitchhikers must be a nuisance, but scientists have never found one in a shark's stomach. They've been found attached to the inside of a shark's mouth, but it seems the smaller fish was never invited to dinner.

Scientists say symbiosis involves both a mutually beneficial relationship and the dissimilarity of the two organisms. Symbiosis is not only found in the ocean. It's a growth force used for spiritual health in the lives of Christians. We can experience mutual benefit in various relationships with people and organizations different from us.

We tend to gravitate toward people like us, and in doing so, we miss out. Sometimes this pull might even be considered a sin, such as prejudice. Do you remember the disagreement between Peter and Paul? Read Galatians 2:11-12 on the next page.

Paul called out Peter (Cephas) for hypocrisy. Peter refused to eat with the Gentiles when other Jews showed up, though he'd been enjoying rich fellowship earlier. Why would Paul publicly humiliate Peter and risk a broken relationship?

*He want Peter to
realize ~~the~~ sin of
prejudice*

Galatians 2:11-12

But when Cephas came to Antioch, I opposed him to his face, because he stood condemned. 12 For prior to the coming of certain men from James, he used to eat with the Gentiles; but when they came, he *began* to withdraw and hold himself aloof, fearing the party of the circumcision.

Prejudice is sin. Period. Our love for one another, regardless of skin color or background, is a solid witness to the gospel's authenticity. It's also a way for us to enjoy symbiotic relationships. People just like us never bring up issues that make us uncomfortable. They don't stretch our thinking and challenge some things we may consider core to our faith.

How do you define prejudice?

Looking at people & think they are Not like you.

Dictionary.com defines prejudice as "an unfavorable opinion or feeling formed beforehand or without knowledge, thought, or reason." It would be like a remora having critical thoughts about a shark before attaching itself to the larger creature. To our detriment, we do it all the time.

We shy away from people of other races or religious backgrounds. Christians, for some reason, have developed this competition-type mentality that says the church down the street is on the other team. They're not! We're on the same team. Satan's our opponent.

Granted, some churches deny the deity of Christ and refuse to accept the Bible as the Word of God, but many Christians share similar beliefs with you. We can have mutually beneficial relationships with believers who are different from us.

This symbiotic relationship can also be experienced in your church. Do you know someone in your church who is different from you? If not, you're not trying hard enough to meet people. Senior adults are different from Gen Zs, and northerners probably have different perspectives on some things than southerners. New Christians are different from mature Christians, and extroverts differ from introverts.

How do you define fellowship? Spoiler alert: it has nothing to do with coffee and donuts.

sharing with all —

The New Testament word for fellowship comes from a Greek word that means sharing—you might even say sharing across boundary lines. God loves diversity. Think about who happened to be in Jerusalem at the time of Pentecost and experienced this kind of fellowship (Acts 2:9-11 gives a list). Read Acts 2:42-47 and write examples of this mutually benefiting relationship in the space below.

Acts 2:42-45

They were continually devoting themselves to the apostles' teaching and to fellowship, to the breaking of bread and to prayer. [43] Everyone kept feeling a sense of awe; and many wonders and signs were taking place through the apostles. [44] And all those who had believed were together and had all things in common; [45] and they *began* selling their property and possessions and were sharing them with all, as anyone might have need.

How do you cross the barrier to beginning one of these symbiotic relationships? It could be with someone of a different race, religious background, or spiritual gift.

Notice the first century believers were devoted to the Word of God and prayer. That's always a good place to start. Suppose your symbiotic relationship is with a Christian from another denomination. Study what you believe and why you believe it and prepare for great conversations in the future with your friend. You'll also understand his perspectives a little better and possibly be stronger in your own beliefs. Regardless of the reason for the diversity, it just takes a little initiative to develop a deep, life-changing friendship.

One great symbiotic relationship can come from two people with different spiritual gifts working together. We'll talk more about spiritual gifts on days eighteen and nineteen, but gift diversity is essential for a healthy church. How could someone with the gift of serving and one with a gift of teaching provide mutual benefit to one another?

_____

_____

_____

Another great diverse relationship can be between two people with different Bible study habits. I have friends who are heavy theological thinkers and others who focus more on personal application. Both are essential. You can learn from other people Bible study habits that will significantly benefit you. You may not ever use your friend's exact method, but that method may inspire you to tweak your strategy for greater benefit.

We could say so much about generational diversity and worship style diversity. Other than Jesus, no one has the corner on the best approach to church or the Christian life. Let's all learn from one another and show grace toward one another. We'll find that kind of relationship will unleash unbelievable power that will lead to fantastic growth in our lives and churches.

Personal Reflection:

- Have you ever had a symbiotic (mutually beneficial) relationship with another person? How was it mutually beneficial? How was the person different from you? *Black / white - teen / 45 yr old* ✗

- Have you struggled with prejudice toward another race or denomination? Confess your bias to God and ask Him to help you overcome this sin. *No, My Mom taught me to* †

- Think of people in your life with whom you can build symbiotic/ *me* relationships. Maybe it's with a senior adult or a teenager. Per- *a very busy* haps this person is charismatic, while you are more mainline. How might this relationship strengthen your church? What steps will you take to build this relationship over the following weeks?

- Write a prayer expressing your desire to experience God's power, creativity, and uniqueness through a mutually beneficial relationship with another believer. Commit to start the process this week.

✗ √ VBS - Black / White Kid / Old

† occational I was prejudiced ("bad ~ Me teeth)

but I still liked them

Day Fourteen

Bearing Fruit

This is to my Father's glory, that you bear much fruit,
showing yourselves to be my disciples. John 15:8

God created a planet on which everything exists to bear fruit. He made all living things to be fruitful and called believers to be fruit bearers. If we're not producing fruit, we're not fulfilling God's purpose. He created a world to produce fruit that provides food, energy, and life for all living things. He produces spiritual fruit in believers and tells us to give it away freely because there is no end to its provision.

As fruit bearers, God calls us to multiplication and high production yields (Jn 15:8). He wants much fruit on the vines of our lives, and the quantity and quality of the fruit should glorify the Father. It's not that we are bearing fruit by our strength but through communion with the Holy Spirit.

This process is natural for believers in Christ, just as for the farmer who plants his fields with seed, which matures and produces the desired crop. Believers are sowing seeds through God's work in their lives, such as godly attitudes, right choices, healthy lifestyles, God-honoring testimonies, and good works. God has chosen us to be fruit bearers, and we are responsible to remain in Christ so we may bear fruit (Jn 15:4).

Believers are not alone. God's enabling grace and power make it possible to be fruit bearers. Grace has enabled us to be a branch, and we produce fruit. It's the life, or sap, of the vine that allows the branch to bloom. The work (power) of the Father through pruning and care enables the vine and allows the branch to produce much fruit. The life-giving power at work is in the fruit where the seed is born, and spiritual nutrition is available to all who taste and see (Psalm 34:8).

We remain in Christ by agreeing to walk with Him, and through His invitation to join Him, we have become conduits for His grace to work for His purposes. Only by grace can we remain in Him and bear fruit as He works in us. We are in Him as He is in us, so we are enabled to serve (empowered) as a kind of spiritual farmer or laborer in a world ready for a great harvest (Mt 9:37).

We glorify God, and the world recognizes who Jesus is through the fruit we bear. As people recognize a tree by its fruit, they recognize followers of Jesus by our fruit. (Mt 12:33). Unbelievers can distinguish the fruit of a tree because God has placed a longing in their hearts for fruit in their lives. All of us desire love, peace, and joy.

What we have in Christ is different from anything most people can imagine. It's not the kind of fruit the world gives but something special from Christ (Jn 14:27).

What kind of fruit are you bearing, and from what tree does it come? Are you bearing something in your flesh, out of pride, greed, or earthly recognition? Or do you bear fruit in the Spirit? Think of examples of both kinds of fruit in your life and write them below.

> *I've done it out of pride or recognition*
> *I hope I have given the " " +*
> *Now bear fruit in the spirit*

Ephesians 5:18	
And do not get drunk with wine, for that is dissipation, but be filled with the Spirit.	Read Ephesians 5:18. Why did Paul contrast drunkenness with being filled with the Spirit? What does this comparison have to do with bearing fruit?

> *drunkenness - can't have*

Jesus said we bear fruit only if we remain in Him (Jn 15:4). He reminds us the Father is pruning the branch, so we'll bear more fruit. Jesus said we have been born again and given the Holy Spirit who works in us to bear much fruit. The Holy Spirit came at Pentecost to empower the disciples to be fruit bearers (Acts 1:8). Jesus promised He'd give power to the disciples when the Holy Spirit came upon them to be witnesses to the world. That promise is true for us as well. The church began to bear much fruit through the presence and work of the Holy Spirit.

God bears fruit in our lives through many means, some of which are listed below:

- the fruit of the Spirit, which is the character of Christ at work through us (Gal 5:22-23)

- evangelism, which is the power of God to change the heart of everyone (Rom 1:16)

- the word of God, which is quick and powerful and when sown brings forth much fruit (Heb 4:12)

- authentic worship, which is the fruit of our lips (Heb 13:15)

- life-changing ministry, which is serving the "least of these," and by doing so, we are serving Christ (Mt 25:31-36)

- Spirit-empowered gifts, which allows the church to be effective and fruitful (Rom 12:3-13).

The Bible gives us many ways to bear fruit, and by this fruit, we show God's power as a demonstration of His presence and a witness to unbelievers.

We live out our calling as Kingdom citizens and administer grace God has freely given us. We have the living water of God's Spirit flowing through the vine and into the branches that bear fruit for God's glory. We are blessed and cannot say we produced the fruit. God produced it because we are part of the vine and because the Father, who is the gardener, is pruning the branches so we are productive (Jn 15:1-2). As we bear fruit, we give others what God has given to us. Fruit is multiplied by sharing.

Personal Reflection

- Do you want to bear much fruit for God? Yes

- What kind of fruit are you bearing? ?

- Can you describe how God has pruned your life to help you bear much fruit?

- What kind of fruit is your church bearing, and how can you help your church become productive through your gifts?
- Express your desire to bear fruit by writing a prayer. Ask God to show you ways fruit can be born through your life and hindrances that may keep you from it.

(Lord help me see how I
can get ways fruit)

Quality Characteristics

We live in a society where everything seems to be instantly available. We expect everyone to be accessible through cell phones, we microwave our food in seconds, and we anticipate two-day delivery from Amazon, maybe sooner.

We expect everything to be instant, but spiritual growth and health aren't. Spiritual health requires a multifaceted approach and regular monitoring. A consistent investment of time and energy yields abundant spiritual fruit, but a lackadaisical approach causes us to fall short of lasting spiritual health.

This investment necessitates understanding eight essential qualities that yield spiritual fortitude:

- Empowering Leadership,
- Gift-based Ministry,
- Passionate Spirituality,
- Effective Structures,
- Inspiring Worship,
- Holistic Small Groups,
- Need-oriented Evangelism,
- Loving Relationships.

We created this study to coexist with a church-wide campaign focusing on church health where we use a process developed by an organization called Natural Church Development (NCD). We've determined the principles leading to healthy churches will also lead to healthy Christians.

NCD has studied close to 100,000 churches worldwide to determine the qualities leading to a healthy church. Although healthy churches grow numerically, the initial approach focused on qualities that made them healthy. Naturally, the qualities leading to health are solid biblical principles every church should implement. Individual believers should also apply these qualities. Most of them are easily transferred to a personal application, but some require more thought.

As you work through the next section, you'll notice we devote two days to each quality. The first day will focus on the ministry area, and the second day will focus on the description. You'll see the corporate application to your local church when you see the ministry areas. Don't stop with the corporate application. Think of the personal application as well.

Considering the biblical concepts behind the larger ministry focus is important. For example, the section dealing with holistic small groups leads you to look at the value of Christian community. For gift-based ministry, reflect on your ministry area and the gifts that make your service possible. Work through each quality and consider the spiritual disciplines, relationships, and practices that will strengthen each quality in your life.

If you are doing this study in conjunction with a health evaluation of your church, you'll see how your application of these qualities will strengthen your church. Even if your church is not participating in a spiritual health evaluation, note how your personal health helps your church be more vital and bear more kingdom fruit.

You should also be able to connect specific spiritual habits or disciplines to each quality. Although prayer and Bible study tie into each quality, you will see how they support passionate spirituality. Service and stewardship connect to gift-based ministry. Effective structures will not only make you think of church systems needed for effective ministry but also will allow your mind to think about personal structures needed to bear fruit. Process each quality in this fashion.

As you study the eight qualities, some will be stronger than others. Try to determine what may be your weakest quality. We call this a minimum factor when helping churches evaluate their health. What will you do to strengthen your minimum factor? Consider ways to use your strengths to bolster your weaknesses.

Finally, just because one area happens to be your strength today doesn't mean it will be your area of strength six months from now. Spiritual health must become a daily focus. Just like you can't eat a healthy meal today for next week, physical, and spiritual health requires daily attention.

As you prepare to look at the eight quality characteristics, consider the words of 2 Peter 1:8: "For if you possess these qualities in increasing measure, they will keep you from being ineffective and unproductive in your knowledge of our Lord Jesus Christ."

Day Fifteen

Empowering *Leadership*

You may be looking at a study on leadership and wonder if this lesson applies to you. It does. Sometimes, leadership is an expression of our gift or position, while other times, it's an overflow of our discipleship. The fact is everyone is a leader at some level at some time. It's that leadership I want to address today.

Years ago, pollster George Barna said, "The American church is dying due to a lack of strong leadership. In this time of unprecedented opportunity and plentiful resources, the church is actually losing influence. The primary reason is the lack of leadership."[1] His comments had an American focus, but we'll discover leadership deficiencies around the globe.

Lack of leadership is prevalent not only in the church but also in secular establishments. We see its effects in the family, schools, and government. As Christians, we need to see leadership as a part of our calling. When I say that, you may think of your pastor, a CEO, or the governor and decide leadership is not a part of your calling. Leadership happens at many levels, and at least one of those levels involves you.

You've probably heard leadership defined at its most basic level as influence. My favorite leadership definition comes from Henry and Richard Blackaby: "Spiritual leadership is moving people on to God's agenda."[2] Do you agree every Christian should be in the business of moving people on to God's agenda? Of course we should. What are some examples of this type of leadership?

Read 2 Timothy 1:5. What two leaders did he mention?

Lois and Eunice

> ### 2 Timothy 1:5
>
> For I am mindful of the sincere faith within you, which first dwelt in your grandmother Lois and your mother Eunice, and I am sure that *it is* in you as well.

I wonder if sweet Lois and Eunice ever considered themselves leaders. Maybe not, but they were. Didn't they help move Timothy on to God's agenda? Parenting and grandparenting are two of the most significant leadership roles in society. Mother's Day and Father's Day are times we honor moms and dads, but it should also be a time for parents to recommit themselves to the leadership task of moving their children on to God's agenda.

Who comes to mind when I mention the name Ananias? The first person who pops into my head is the man, along with his wife, Sapphira, who tried to deceive the early church in Acts 5. The second one is found in Acts 23-24 and was the High Priest when the religious leaders brought Paul before the Sanhedrin in Jerusalem.

It's the third Ananias I want us to consider. Read Acts 9:10-14.

Acts 9:10-14

Now there was a disciple at Damascus named Ananias; and the Lord said to him in a vision, "Ananias." And he said, "Here I am, Lord." ¹¹ And the Lord *said* to him, "Get up and go to the street called Straight, and inquire at the house of Judas for a man from Tarsus named Saul, for he is praying, ¹² and he has seen in a vision a man named Ananias come in and lay his hands on him, so that he might regain his sight." ¹³ But Ananias answered, "Lord, I have heard from many about this man, how much harm he did to Your saints at Jerusalem; ¹⁴ and here he has authority from the chief priests to bind all who call on Your name."

Do you consider Ananias to be a leader? Would you say God used him to move someone on to God's agenda?   Yes

Isn't it amazing God came to Ananias to send him to a particular address on Earth? Every time I read that story, I'm reminded God knows where I am. God knew where Saul was, and God knew where Ananias was. He knows where you are. You may be in the right place serving the Lord or running from God, like Jonah did. You may be so focused on changing diapers you haven't thought about the future godly leader in front of you with diaper rash. God knows where you are, and He's ready to help you get to where He wants you.

These verses point out Ananias was a reluctant leader. Why was he reluctant?

He was worried others would accept Saul (later Paul)

Do you blame him? Saul was known to be a Christian killer. Going to Straight Street would have been dangerous for any Christian, and God was telling Ananias to visit Saul. Has God ever given you a difficult assignment? Were you listening? *Evidently not*

One assignment He is giving you is to influence others for the Kingdom of God. Whether you lead a large organization or stand in front of multitudes is beside the point. Your leadership might be similar to a sweet elderly gentleman on my paper route. When I was a teenager, Mr. Ben Gatlin often told me he prayed for me every day. I was a fifteen-year-old kid, and he was probably in his eighties. He knew me by name and helped move me on to God's agenda.

Think of people from your past who led you on to God's agenda. How did they do it?

Grand fannie, Mother, Candice Moore (Mentor), & More

What's wrong with Ananias' response?

He was not depending on God & lack of faith

It does show a lack of faith and a bit of presumption. Isn't it amazing how we often think God needs our help to do things?

Read the rest of the story in Acts 9:15-18. In verse fifteen, God told Ananias, "Go; he is a chosen instrument of mine." What would have happened if Ananias had been disobedient? He would have missed out on being a part of something incredible. Have you ever said no to God? Write about it below:

Yes, I was afraid to witness at times (Jerry Spencer)

God wants you to be willing to step up and lead. If you are going to be a healthy Christian, you need to fulfill your calling to be a godly influence. You have a role in your church's health as well. Are you willing to tell one of your church leaders you are available to serve?

Tomorrow, we'll focus on the principle of empowering leadership and focus on the empowering part. Your church leaders are looking for people they can empower to carry out the work and mission of the church. Will you step forward and be a part of what God is doing in the church? The world? What if He's calling *you* to go to "Straight Street?" Will you be obedient?

Personal Reflection

- Reread the two definitions of leadership above. How has God used you to influence others and move others on to His agenda?

- Make a list of all the leaders God has used in your life. Remember, some of them might not seem like leaders, but God used them in a leadership role. Why not send them a note thanking them for their godly influence on your life? *Done*

- Is it possible God has a chosen instrument in mind, and He wants you to lead them on to God's agenda? What ways are you already doing that now? *S.S., God's Girl, Nursery, VBS*

- Write a prayer expressing your willingness to be a leader for God's glory.

Scripture Memory Verse

Galatians 2:20 "I have been crucified with Christ; and it is no longer I who live, but Christ lives in me; and the *life* which I now live in the flesh I live by faith in the Son of God, who loved me and gave Himself up for me."

Day Sixteen

Empowering Leadership

You will find many types of leaders in healthy and unhealthy churches. In studying thousands of healthy churches worldwide, Christian Schwarz made an important discovery. Healthy churches not only require leaders; they require empowering leaders.

Notice I didn't say "empowered leaders." What's the difference between empowered leaders and empowering leaders?

Done / Needs Work

Ephesians 4:11-12
And He gave some *as* apostles, and some *as* prophets, and some *as* evangelists, and some *as* pastors and teachers, ¹² for the equipping of the saints for the work of service, to the building up of the body of Christ.

Ephesians 4:11-12 provides an example of empowering leaders.

When I first studied this passage many years ago in the KJV, the translators included a comma in verse twelve after the word "saints." It said God gave various leaders to the church for the "perfecting of the saints, for the work of the ministry, for the edifying of the body of Christ." Keep in mind the original Greek New Testament did not include commas. Translators or editors added them to make reading easier. In this case, however, commas changed the meaning of the text. Read the two versions and describe the difference.

_____

_____

_____

Do you see the subtle difference? The biblical record is clear that God gave leaders to equip believers for the work of ministry. This truth is the whole point of spiritual gifts. It reminds us God called every Christian to serve.

A healthy church will have leaders who empower others to serve. Schwarz said empowering leaders explain, motivate, and liberate other leaders. What does this statement mean? It means ministry is shared. It means healthy Christian leaders are never content to do the work alone. You'd never hear a healthy leader say, "If you want something done right, do it yourself." Such words come from insecure leaders, not biblical leaders.

What does this concept of empowering mean to you as an individual Christian? The application will be expressed differently depending upon your leadership role, but it begins with a mentality shift. We shift from seeing the church run by experts to seeing leaders who work themselves out of a job. These healthy leaders train people to take over what they are doing so the leaders can focus on something else.

Moses had to make this shift. Read Exodus 18:1-27. It records the story of Moses' father-in-law, Jethro, coming to visit and seeing Moses doing all the leadership work. Why not? He was the anointed, the professional leader, the one most qualified. The "Why not?" is because he was killing himself with the workload and robbing others of the joy of using their gifts. Jethro gave him a delegation principle that made the workload more manageable.

What is the empowering principle Jethro challenged Moses to implement?

Group of 10 for each leader

Think about people you influence or should be influencing. How can you empower them to lead and serve? Consider this example: let's say you are a parent, and you lead your family devotions three times a week. What if your oldest son is twelve, and your middle child, a daughter, is eight. You could share the leadership responsibilities by teaching your twelve-year-old to lead devotions. Get him to involve his sister by having her read the scripture. Your youngest can lead a song. You can lead twice a week, and your children can lead the other time.

Jimmy → I failed at 11
have devotion

How can you be an empowering leader to your friends at church, at work, or in the community? Think of an example and write it below.

S.S. – Encourage class to take other "jobs" are done

Barnabas is an example of an empowering leader. The book of Acts doesn't give us all the details, but we see the overwhelming result of his actions. In Acts 13, we read where God called the church to set apart Paul and Barnabas for the missionary journey. Read verse five to see who accompanied them.

Acts 13:5 When they reached Salamis, they *began* to proclaim the word of God in the synagogues of the Jews; and they also had John as their helper.

The "John" mentioned in the verse is John Mark, cousin to Barnabas. Notice what happened when they left Paphos as recorded in verse thirteen: "Now Paul and his companions put out to sea from Paphos and came to Perga in Pamphylia, but John left them and returned to Jerusalem."

Some say Mark left because he got homesick, while others think he couldn't handle the rigors of living on the road. We don't know the real answer, but his departure caused a problem when it was time to go on a second missionary journey. Read about it in Acts 15:37-40.

Acts 15:37-40

Barnabas wanted to take John, called Mark, along with them also. 38 But Paul kept insisting that they should not take him along who had deserted them in Pamphylia and had not gone with them to the work. 39 And there occurred such a sharp disagreement that they separated from one another, and Barnabas took Mark with him and sailed away to Cyprus. 40 But Paul chose Silas and left, being committed by the brethren to the grace of the Lord.

Wow. Paul, the great missionary, had a blowout with his faithful friend, Barnabas. It was such a blowout that they parted ways, and we never hear from Barnabas (whose name means "son of encouragement") again.

By the time Paul was under house arrest in Rome, we can read between the lines and note something significant had happened. Read 2 Timothy 4:11.

You may not know of Mark as the young man who abandoned Paul and Barnabas or the one Paul asked to visit him in Rome.

> **2 Timothy 4:11**
>
> Only Luke is with me. Pick up Mark and bring him with you, for he is useful to me for service.

What's the main thing we know about Mark? *He went on a second missio He was John Mark*

Did you say he wrote the second gospel? Many scholars think Mark's gospel was the earliest and became the model the others followed in telling the story of Jesus.

God's hand Wouldn't you have loved to have watched Barnabas, the son of encouragement, empowering broken Mark for ministry? Somehow, Mark went from being useless to being useful to the great Apostle Paul. Thankfully, Paul was willing to eat a little humble pie. How did this transformation happen? Empowering leadership. Barnabas turned failure into success. We would never have known Mark, but now, we know him better than we know Barnabas.

If you are going to be a healthy Christian, and part of a healthy church, you need to be an empowering leader. Look for people you can encourage, equip, and set free to serve.

Personal Reflection

- Make a list of people you are empowering or should be empowering to lead.

- What are significant challenges you'll encounter as you empower others for the work of ministry?

- How can you empower through your role as a parent, friend, or coworker?
- Write a prayer expressing your willingness to be an empowering leader. You may need to confess your sin of selfishness for trying to do it all in the past. Ask God to help you to become an effective, empowering leader with your children, spouse, friends, and fellow believers.

Lord, help me to be an example to my Children + G'ch + other family members —

Help me to be an example for all. Let people see Christus in me —

Gift-based *Ministry*

*As each one has received a special gift, employ it in serving one another
as good stewards of the manifold grace of God.*
1 Peter 4:10

We've all seen the shows or commercials where someone performs some death-defying deed, but beforehand, he warns viewers, "Don't try this at home." Many Christians view ministry this way. I remember being told in my first church I couldn't baptize someone until I'd been ordained. Really? Where is that in the Bible? Many believed baptizing was reserved only for the professionals, the ordained—"Don't try this at home."

We need to be careful about distinguishing between professional ministers and mere mortals. This distinction grew in popularity during a period in church history known as the dark ages. The Bible makes no distinction between clergy and lay people. The Greek word translated *laity* means *all the people*. I'm part of the laity, even though I'm an ordained clergyman.

When Peter wrote to the early church, he told the believers they had received a special gift. Look at the following six words after *gift*. God calls Christians to "employ it in serving one another." The Greek word for serving is the same word from which we get our English word deacon or minister. We are to use our gifts to minister to one another.

Serving is not just for the professionals. It's for all the people of God. Pastor and author Rick Warren is fond of saying, "Every member is a minister."

Notice when we serve one another, we are good stewards of God's manifold grace. As believers use their unique ways of serving, those acts of ministry will look different from acts of other believers, and their service will be an act of stewarding God's grace. Our service looks different because our gifts are different. If we don't minister to others, we are poor stewards of God's gifts and opportunities.

Ephesians 2:8-9 reminds us we are saved by grace through faith. Our works have nothing to do with earning salvation. You can't earn it, so you can't boast about your works. The next verse puts works into perspective. Read Ephesians 2:10.

> **Ephesians 2:10**
>
> For we are His workmanship, created in Christ Jesus for good works, which God prepared beforehand so that we would walk in them.

Why can't we boast about our works? Reread the first phrase of Ephesians 2:10 aloud and emphasize the word *His*.

Workmanship could be translated a *work of art* or even a *poem*. When we look at a masterpiece by a famous artist, we know the painting didn't paint itself, so ultimately, the artist receives the glory.

This verse also underscores our purpose. What did God plan for us beforehand?

__What good works we would do__

Doing good works is an expression of our design. Our Designer wrote good works into our DNA before we were created. What do you think the Apostle Paul meant when he wrote the word *beforehand* in Ephesians 2:10? Before you were born? Before your parents were born? Is it possible God had you in mind and had a plan for your life when He made the world?

Regardless of the timing of His plans, it was, at least, before you were born. God designed you for good works. He made you to serve others and to serve Himself.

Many studies show we function best when we serve others. Psychologist Elizabeth Hopper wrote, "Being kind and helpful can make us happier, give us a sense of purpose and meaning, and even lower our blood pressure. People across cultures seem to experience greater well-being when they help others, suggesting this may be a human universal."[1] Isn't it interesting to read a secular psychologist tell us human beings were designed for good works?

One study published in the *Journal of Experimental Social Psychology* revealed even people who have committed crimes feel good when they give to others.[2] Thieves who take from others feel better when they give to people. Interesting.

When Paul reminded us God planned ahead of time the good works we should do, he ended the sentence by saying, "so we should walk in them." He's saying, "God made you to do good works, so do good works." The word *walk* comes from a Greek compound word meaning *walk about*. God is saying as you walk about in life, do what you were made to do: serve others in Jesus' name. We were made to minister.

One reason ministering to others brings such personal benefit, especially for Christians, is we connect to God's work in the world. Whenever I help someone through a personal witness, a word of encouragement, or meeting a physical need, I know I am connecting my life to God's grand design for the world. I'm not just marking time or treading water; instead, I'm doing something that matters and lasts for eternity.

Ministering to others is also an act of worship. Read Romans 12:1. When you think of sacrifices in the Old Testament, you think of something God's followers killed. Why does God want our bodies as living sacrifices?

> **Romans 12:1**
> Therefore I urge you, brethren, by the mercies of God, to present your bodies a living and holy sacrifice, acceptable to God, *which is* your spiritual service of worship.

To serve God & Hers
as we worship God

God points out our living sacrifice of service is a service of worship. This truth means when you minister by teaching a group of children, changing diapers in the nursery, or feeding the hungry, you worship God or draw attention to "the Artist."

When we think of a minister, we usually envision the pastor preaching a sermon or providing care amid a crisis. Of course, that's ministry, but so is cleaning your elderly neighbor's gutters, organizing food at the local food pantry, and taking a meal to a grieving family.

Health is at the forefront of people's minds. People spend a lot of money to pay for gym memberships and personal trainers. Health, however, is multifaceted and must include physical, spiritual, and emotional well-being. If you want to be healthy, minister to others. Ministering's not just for professionals. It's also for you. Ignore the warnings or unbiblical distinctions. Try it at home, at church, and in your neighborhood. You'll be thrilled you did.

Personal Reflection

- Do you draw distinctions between the professional clergy and the rest of the church? Why do you think Christians create this difference? Is the distinction biblical? So we have a leader

- What is your reaction to Ephesians 2:10, which says we are God's workmanship or work of art? How do you feel about God designing you for a purpose? I Know He did

- Are you fulfilling your purpose in ministry? If not, what needs to change? ? Time for me to chang ? ?

- How does knowing your acts of service are acts of worship change how you may serve in the future?

- Write a prayer expressing your desire to serve. Tell God your hesitations or fears. Are you willing to tell Him you'll be a minister by fulfilling the purpose for which He made you?

Day Eighteen

Gift-based Ministry

For just as we have many members in one body and all the members do not have the same function,⁵ so we, who are many, are one body in Christ, and individually members one of another.
Romans 12:4-5

How proficient are you at putting square pegs into round holes? You're probably as ineffective as the rest of us, yet many of us attempt the challenge when we volunteer for ministry for which God never equipped us or called us.

Have you ever tried to do something you weren't equipped to do? It's like trying to drive nails with a pair of pliers. You may eventually get the nail into the wood, but you'd be frustrated from the effort, and it would take days for your hands to recover. You'd never volunteer for nail driving again.

Church leaders may ask us to do ministry tasks we have no business attempting. Imagine putting an introvert at the front door as a greeter or an expressive extrovert in with the bed babies while they're napping. Although understanding personalities is helpful in finding our place of ministry, God has given us a greater resource to help us see where He planned for us to serve: spiritual gifts.

Scripture tells us God has given us at least one spiritual gift to use in ministry. Spiritual gifts are God-empowered abilities God gives Christians for the purpose of serving Him. We don't earn or deserve them, so they're called gifts. The Bible uses a Greek word for spiritual gifts that could be translated as *grace gifts*.

You can find a list of these gifts in Romans 12:6-8, 1 Corinthians 12:8-10, and Ephesians 4:11. In 1 Corinthians 7:7, you'll also find the word "grace gift" used to describe the gift of celibacy. Could our list of spiritual gifts in Scripture be inconclusive? Possibly.

However, since God wants us to understand our gifts, it seems He'd provide a complete explanation. Regardless, these passages are a great place to start.

Read 1 Corinthians 12:4-6. Do you notice repetition of the word "varieties"? You could translate the word as "different." What does this passage say we have varieties of?

1 Corinthians 12:4-6

Now there are varieties of gifts, but the same Spirit. [5] And there are varieties of ministries, and the same Lord. [6] There are varieties of effects, but the same God who works all things in all persons.

gifts, ministries

God gives different gifts for various ministries with diverse effects. This passage means God may provide the same gift to several people, and they will use that gift in different ministries. It's also possible God will gift others, and they will use those gifts in the same ministry. For example, a Christian counselor could have the gift of encouragement or the gift of teaching. How would those ministries be different based on the counselor's gifts?

teaching should encourage those being taught

We see this difference all the time in pastors of churches. Some have gifts of teaching, while others have gifts of exhortation, or even something else. While gifts have various uses, you will benefit from understanding your gift and knowing how to use it in your ministry. Your ministry will have different effects based on your gift. The key to this is God has gifted you and will work through you as you use your gift for His glory.

Sadly, most Christians don't understand this truth. Many Christians volunteer to serve in a particular area simply because there's a need. That's not a good enough reason. My mother used to say, "If you're not you, who's going to be you?" She was telling me not to be someone I'm not. Christians often take on responsibilities for things they're not gifted for, and because they're busy trying to put a square peg in a round hole, they don't have the time or energy to do the things God made them to do.

Yesterday's study mentioned finding happiness through serving. However, we find our greatest joy when we serve according to our spiritual gifts. When you participate in a ministry where your gift is employed, you will enjoy supernatural fruit that comes through God's Spirit. As a Christian, one of the greatest joys is to know God is working through your life and ministry to make an eternal difference.

You will find numerous resources online or in books that can help you figure out your gift(s). Christian Schwarz wrote *The 3 Colors of Ministry*, which offers an excellent online gift assessment. If you Google "spiritual gift profile," you'll discover additional resources from sites like lifeway.com, churchgrowth.org, and uniquelyyou.org.

Here's a helpful process you can follow to determine your spiritual gift(s):

1) Study the gift list from Scripture and pick two or three you think connect with your passions.
2) Talk with close friends about your opinion and see if they agree.
3) Find a good assessment and complete it.
4) Pick your top gift and volunteer to serve short-term in an area where you can use that gift.
5) Evaluate your ministry and look for spiritual fruit. Include friends in this process.

Sometimes, we're blind to our strengths or weaknesses. When I was a minister of education years ago, one of my most significant challenges was to help someone understand she didn't have the gift of teaching even though she thought she did.

One gift is not greater than another. All gifts are needed. You'll find joy and spiritual health when you determine your gift(s) and use them meaningfully. You should think about your gift and consider how you can help your church family engage their gifts in ministry. Developing a gift-based ministry as a believer and as a church will change your life and church and impact the world for eternity.

Personal Reflection

- Have you ever tried to perform a ministry you know you were not gifted or equipped to do? What was it like? Did you enjoy it or simply endure it? *I thought teaching – but a test so, d*
- Do you know your spiritual gift(s)? What's the benefit of focusing on the ministry God has gifted you to do?
- What are ways you can help your church members employ a gift-based ministry? *7*
- Write a prayer asking God to help you discern your gift(s) and determine the best way to use it (them). Express your willingness to help your church pursue a ministry strategy that includes assisting others in learning their gifts and using them in fruit-bearing ministry.

Day Nineteen

Passionate *Spirituality*

Passionate spirituality should be a quality characteristic of healthy churches and healthy Christians, but what is it? The word *spirituality* is applied to many different areas in our society, so agreeing on an acceptable definition is essential.

If you Google the word *spirituality*, you'll find the primary definition is being connected to something bigger than ourselves. Websites dealing with spirituality cover psychological well-being, eastern religions, new age thought, astrology, meditation, natural healing, mediums, and similar topics. Sites with a solid Christian message are difficult to find.

Although the vague definition mentioned above is accurate, we must define what "something bigger" is. True spirituality can't mean defining that "something" according to our wishes, understanding, or experiences. The something bigger is a Someone bigger, Jesus, and He died on a cross so you could experience spirituality at its greatest.

Our spirituality points to a connection to our Creator. Jesus spoke with a Jewish leader named Nicodemus about this connection. Read John 3:5-7. How did Jesus describe this spiritual transformation? He spoke of two different births. What were they, and what did He mean?

We've heard the words "born again" used so often that many have not thought about the seriousness of their meaning. Jesus referred to our moment of salvation as being born again, a second birth into God's family. Our second birth is spiritual,

> **John 3:5-7**
>
> Jesus answered, "Truly, truly, I say to you, unless one is born of water and the Spirit he cannot enter into the kingdom of God. ⁶ That which is born of the flesh is flesh, and that which is born of the Spirit is spirit. ⁷ Do not be amazed that I said to you, 'You must be born again.'"

a spiritual connection that forever links our spirits with the Spirit of God and God's family.

Although God establishes this connection at a Christian's second birth, Christian spirituality is about growing in our relationship with Jesus and experiencing God daily in fresh, meaningful ways. It's daily living in the presence of God and walking consistently in surrender to God's Holy Spirit.

Jesus used imagery of a vine (Him) and branches (believers) to talk about staying connected. Read John 15:5. What key word did He use to describe this connection? What is the result of this connection?

> **John 15:5**
>
> I am the vine, you are the branches; he who abides in Me and I in him, he bears much fruit, for apart from Me you can do nothing.

abias in Him

We've spent a day focusing on fruitfulness. I want you to focus specifically on the word *abides*. What do you think Jesus meant by using that word?

living in —

The Greek word translated as *abide* is used in a form that points to continuous action. The definition of the word underscores that truth as well. As a branch, we must stay connected to the vine.

Not only are we connected to Christ, but also we are connected to the body of Christ. Part of our spirituality is knowing we are connected to others and living out that community in meaningful ways. Think about the "one another" commands in the Bible: love one another, serve one another, encourage one another, etc. You'll find one of my favorites in Hebrews 10:24-25 printed on the next page. What are the two "one another" commands in those verses?

Instead of "stimulate," as in the New American Standard Version, the King James Version of the Bible uses the word "provoke." The Greek word describes what you do with a cattle prod. Sounds painful. The message of these two verses (stimulate one another to love and good deeds, assemble, encourage one another) points to the necessity of being connected to other believers in meaningful relationships. Do

> **Hebrews 10:24-25**
> and let us consider how to stimulate one another to love and good deeds, 25 not forsaking our own assembling together, as is the habit of some, but encouraging *one another*; and all the more as you see the day drawing near.

you have close relationships with other Christians? What can you do to form those relationships or strengthen ones you already have?

_____

_____

Spirituality is not only about connection; it's also about conforming. God's first goal for us is we be born again. Romans 8:29 reveals a second goal. What is it?

to be more like Jesus

_____

> **Romans 8:29**
> For those whom He foreknew, He also predestined *to become* conformed to the image of His Son, so that He would be the firstborn among many brethren.

Sometimes, people get hung up on the word *foreknew* or *predestined*. The fact God knew in advance who would be saved shouldn't surprise us. God knows everything. Predestined means determined ahead of time. What did God determine ahead of time? Before we were born and even before He created Adam and Eve, God decided He wanted followers of Jesus to be like His Son.

What does it mean to be conformed to Jesus' image?

_____

_____

Did you say something about Christ's character? We can connect God's plan to the fruit of the Spirit and character qualities mentioned in the Beatitudes of the Sermon on the Mount.

If we will live out our spirituality and grow in it as followers of Jesus, there's one final "C" word we can add to *connection* and *conform*: *consistency.* God wants you to consistently grow in your relationship with Him in order to express your ongoing spirituality. The only way a branch can bear fruit is to stay connected to the vine so it can draw nutrients that yield fruit.

Discipline is related to consistency. Some people don't like the word, but it's an integral part to expressing our spirituality. Paul even told young Timothy to "train yourself to be godly." Dallas Willard wrote, "A discipline for the spiritual life is…nothing but an activity undertaken to bring us into more effective cooperation with Christ and his Kingdom." [1]

When you think of spiritual disciplines, what comes to mind?

_____

_____

We can make a list of disciplines. Some that would end up at the top are Bible reading/study, prayer, worship, fasting, and fellowship. Dallas Willard listed fifteen disciplines in his book. John Ortberg focused on ten disciplines in one of my favorite books, "The Life You've Always Wanted." [2]

We are spiritual beings because God breathed into us the breath of life. How you pursue and live out that spirituality is up to you. I once read Christian spirituality involves a choice we make to "know and grow" in our relationships with Jesus. Are you making that choice daily? What are you doing to know and grow in your relationship with Christ?

Personal Reflection

- We don't decide to become spiritual people. We *are* spiritual people. The question is "How well are we expressing our spirituality as followers of Jesus?" On a scale of one to five, with five being the best, how would you rate your connection to God?   *3*   ?

- What are you doing to abide in Christ? Make a list of five things you can do to stay connected to "the Vine."

- Would you say you're more like Jesus today than two years ago? Five years ago? What steps can you take to make sure you are being conformed to the image of Christ?

- Is living out your spirituality consistently a challenge? Write a prayer sharing your thoughts and desire to express your spirituality in God-honoring ways.

Bible reading, S.S., Pray, + Live fr Him +
I like him

Day Twenty

Passionate Spirituality

Bless the Lord, oh my soul, and all that is within me
bless His holy Name. Psalm 103:1

Yesterday, we saw spirituality is *connecting* to God, *conforming* to Christ, and *consistently growing* in our relationships with Jesus. As crucial as our spirituality is to our spiritual health, the word spirituality itself doesn't capture the proper measurement needed to produce fruit in our lives. What kind of spirituality do we need? How much should spirituality describe our lives? We must define spirituality, or we may accept a basic understanding that never leads us to experience a God-honoring, fruit-bearing life.

If spirituality is to be life-changing, it must be passionate. The word passionate may evoke thoughts of romance, but it can be applied to any area of life. In general, passion points to expressing intense feelings. Of course, we can direct those feelings toward another person, but we can also direct them toward sports, politics, or hobbies. In this case, we can be passionate about spirituality.

We can measure passionate spirituality by time in the Word of God and prayer, personal and corporate engagement in worship, and ministry to others. At the same time, a person can spend time reading the Bible and attending worship but still be far from God and not register on a spirituality scale. A passionate relationship with Jesus doesn't come from logging time in the Bible or on a pew (or chairs if you attend my church).

Three words come to mind as I consider how to pursue a passionate spirituality. The first one is *consuming*. Look at the opening scripture from Psalm 103. What word points to being consumed?

all that is in in me

What do you think the psalmist meant by saying he would worship God with all that is within him?   _surrendered_

He would give (surrender) all to Him.

I think of three aspects that define me: <u>mind</u>, <u>will</u>, and <u>emotions</u>. Everyone is different. Some of us are oriented toward emotional worship, while others lean toward a cerebral experience. Some raise their hands, and others sit on them. We all must consider how to bless the Lord with all that is within us. How can I connect <u>my heart and emotions in worshiping Him</u>? Passionate spirituality <u>means I am consumed with my love for God and seek to express it with all my being.</u>

Being consumed also emphasizes the role of the Word of God and the Spirit of God in us. Psalm 119 is an excellent chapter about being saturated in the Word of God and being obedient to its commands. Read Psalm 119:10-11.

Psalm 119:10-11

With all my heart I have sought You; do not let me wander from Your commandments. ¹¹ Your word I have <u>treasured</u> in my <u>heart</u>, that I may not sin against you.

What words or phrases point to passionate spirituality in the psalmist's life?

all my heart I have sought You - Your word I have

The <u>psalmist loved God's Word</u>. We don't know the human author of the psalm or when it was written, but some suggest either David, Ezra, or Daniel. Imagine how thrilled the author would be to have a bound copy of the sixty-six books we enjoy reading as our Bible. What would treasuring God's Word look like to you?

We want to read it again again - memorize all we can

A passionate spirituality is not only consuming but also _dependent._ <u>We are dependent upon the Holy Spirit.</u> Passionate spirituality is grounded in the Word of God and directed by the Spirit of God. Jesus told us the Holy Spirit would teach us all things (Jn 14:26), convict the world of sin, righteousness, and judgment (Jn 14:8), develop our character (Gal 5:22-23), gift us for ministry (1 Cor 12:7), and guide us into all truth (Jn 16:13).

> ### 2 Corinthians 3:15-18
> But to this day whenever Moses is read, a veil lies over their heart; ¹⁶ but whenever a person turns to the Lord, the veil is taken away. ¹⁷ Now the Lord is the Spirit, and where the Spirit of the Lord is, *there* is liberty. ¹⁸ But we all, with unveiled face, beholding as in a mirror the glory of the Lord, are being transformed into the same image from glory to glory, just as from the Lord, the Spirit.

Read 2 Corinthians 3:15-18. The Apostle Paul wrote that many read the first five books of the Old Testament through filters that blocked out the passage's true meaning. When we became followers of Christ, we received the Holy Spirit, and He removed that filter. What do you think he meant when he said we behold the glory of the Lord as in a mirror?

We can see God as he is

Have you ever looked at yourself and thought about God's glory? The only way we reflect God's glory is through the transforming work of the Spirit of God in the context of our passionate spirituality.

One final word connected to passionate spirituality is essential: *interdependent.* This word points to our connection to God's community, the Church. We've written of this truth throughout the book. Healthy Christians do not live out their faith as Lone Rangers. People tell me they don't have to go to church to be a Christian. True. Going to church doesn't make you a Christian, but why wouldn't someone with passionate spirituality want to connect with the family of God?

I tell people you don't have to go to church to be a Christian, but you must go to church to be an obedient Christian (consider all the "one another" commands). I want to take this thought a step further. You cannot have a passionate relationship with Jesus Christ if you are not meaningfully connected to a body of believers seeking to be led by God's Spirit and obedient to His Word.

Are you consumed by your love for God and saturated with the Word of God? Do you love talking to God about anything and everything in your life and world? Do you live every day wanting to be filled and directed by the Spirit of God as you seek to fulfill His mission? The level of your spirituality and the potential of its results will be directly proportionate to how you answer those questions.

Personal Reflection

- Have you ever read the Bible and attended church but still found yourself far from God? We know Bible reading, prayer, and church attendance are important parts of passionate spirituality. How do you turn those actions from a perfunctory, religious ritual into experiences that feed and express your passionate love for Jesus?

- Scan Psalm 119 in your Bible. What phrases catch your attention that you'd like to be true of your experience?

- Do you have life-giving relationships with Christian friends? If not, what's keeping you from pursuing such a relationship? Do you agree these relationships are an integral part of your Christian life? Maybe you attend a small group, but you'd say your group doesn't deepen your faith or stoke your passion. What steps can you take to change that?

- Write a prayer expressing your desire to be consumed by the Word of God and directed by the Spirit of God. Ask God to help you develop a community of Christian friends who help each other experience passionate spirituality.

Effective *Structures*

When you read the words *structures*, *systems*, or *processes*, do your eyes glaze over with disinterest or dread? Or do these words light your fire and cause you to feel giddy with excitement as you make your "to do" list?

Whether we are structured or flexible, organization and processes are essential parts of life. For example, physical health comes in response to an organized body that follows specific processes like clockwork.

Aren't you grateful that about every second, your heart produces a double thud of a beat? This process pushes blood from one chamber to the next and from the lower chamber into your lungs to pick up oxygen. Your oxygen-rich blood then feeds the rest of your body. It's a process or a needed structure that makes your body healthy. If you want to be spiritually healthy, you need spiritual structures in your life.

Read Proverbs 4:20-23 and note the parallels of our physical health to our spiritual health. What does the writer say brings health or life?

> **Proverbs 4:20-23**
> My son, give attention to my words; incline your ear to my sayings. 21 Do not let them depart from your sight; keep them in the midst of your heart. 22 For they are life to those who find them and health to all their body. 23 Watch over your heart with all diligence, for from it *flow* the springs of life.

His words (saying

How do we apply the last verse? How do you watch over your heart spiritually, and what do you think the writer means?

_____

_____

_____

We can find a perfect, symbolic picture of structures needed for spiritual health in the construction of the Old Testament tabernacle. God instructed Moses to erect a rectangular fence of animal skin about eight feet tall. Within this rectangle, God told him to build a smaller rectangular tent with a taller roof, maybe sixteen feet and divided into two sections. The outdoor section surrounded by an eight-foot barrier was called the outer court. The first section of the tent, or smaller rectangle, was named the Holy Place, and the last inner room where the priests kept the Ark of the Covenant was called the Holy of Holies.

Label the symbolism in the drawing below as we look at it in the following sentences. The area outside the tabernacle represents our relationship with the world. The outer court was an area reserved for the Jewish people to bring sacrifices, so let's say it represents our relationship with other Christians or the Church. Once inside the tent, the Holy Place was a smaller area reserved for a small group

The Old Testament Tabernacle

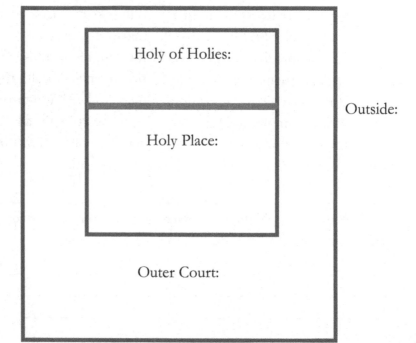

Holy of Holies:

Holy Place:

Outside:

Outer Court:

of priests. This area can be a picture of your deeper relationships with a small group of Christian friends. You may serve together in a particular ministry, even as priests served together in this room.

The last room, the Holy of Holies, was reserved for the High Priest to enter once a year with the annual sacrifice. This room is the place where the High Priest met with God. This final area represents your inner life—the deepest parts of your soul where you encounter God. It's the place where spiritual intimacy is nurtured. If you are going to be spiritually healthy, you need to consider all four aspects or structures in your life.

Let's start with the smallest room, the Holy of Holies. This tiny room points to the place where you encounter God in intimate, personal ways. It's the place of the soul or the inner life. Author Dallas Willard referred to this place as "the hinge on which the rest of your life hangs."

In contrast to the High Priest's annual visit to the Old Testament Holy of Holies, we need to visit this room daily, maybe multiple times a day. Our inner life is the foundation of every aspect of life, and it's the springboard to spiritual health. In Colossians 3:9-10, God reminds us not to lie to one another since we've laid aside the old self "and have put on the new self who is being renewed to a true knowledge according to the image of the One who created him." What does the verse mean to "put on the new self?"

Change myself

How are we renewed? This phrase points to the inner life, the inner connection with our Creator. Throughout the Bible, especially the New Testament, God reminds us being a follower of Jesus is about growing relationships with Him. Would you describe your Christian faith as a growing relationship with Christ? Can you think of some structures or systems you can put in place to strengthen your relationship with Jesus?

Once you leave the Holy of Holies, you step into the room where the priests work in small groups. I'd like this room to remind us of our close connection to a small group of believers. This group consists of people with whom we have a deeper relationship than with anyone else. It would include spouses and family members, but it should also include people in our small group or people we consider accountability or prayer partners. We cannot be spiritually healthy without meaningful, transparent relationships with a few Christians in our lives. Maybe a structure to help in this area could be a commitment to attend a weekly small group meeting. Can you think of others?

The tabernacle's outer court points to our relationship to the larger body of believers we call the church. Technically, this relationship connects us to every Christian on the planet, but specifically, when we join a local congregation, we enter a covenant relationship with that group of believers.

Although I don't know everyone in my church, I am still connected by covenant. I pray for my congregation, and I'd help anyone in my church family. We share the same mission and work together to bear fruit in the world. I'm growing in my friendship with people in my church, and I connect to someone new every week. We are the family of God. My spiritual health will affect the spiritual health of my church. We've said it several times: spiritually healthy churches are made up of spiritually healthy Christians. How can you connect with your church? _I hope I do!_

We have a mandate to connect to those who don't know Christ, so the final area is outside the walls of the tabernacle—the world. Jesus was called a friend of sinners. Are you? Sometimes it's a challenge to be in the world but not of it, but we must be intentional about connecting with unbelievers if we're going to be salt and light.

Healthy Christians are also working to reflect God's character, mission, and justice in a world broken by sin. If our focus is only upon ourselves, we have a spiritual malady. Jesus never focused on Himself.

Consider the structures in your life. Can you imagine yourself functioning in the four areas I've highlighted? In which of those areas do you have the most vital relationship? Which needs more attention?

Small groups

those outside

Personal Reflection

- Are you a structured person, or do you go with the flow? What are the strengths and weaknesses of each?

- Structures are not just important; they're essential. Before you can think about how to make a structure effective, you need to understand how it works and what part it plays in making you holistically healthy. What role does each of the four areas play in your spiritual health?

- You've considered which areas are your strongest and weakest. Write a prayer expressing your desire to strengthen all four areas, especially your weaker ones, and see these areas develop spiritual health in your life. Ask God to show you how your structures fit into the larger system of your church.

Lord, help help me to share Jesus with all!

Day Twenty-two

Effective Structures

Seeing that His divine power has granted to us everything pertaining to life
and godliness, through the true knowledge of Him who called you
by His own glory and excellence. 2 Peter 1:3

Everyone has structures in their lives, but they must be effective structures in order to promote spiritual health.

Have you ever ordered something only to discover it's defective? That problem happened to me recently. I ordered a smartphone holder for my car. It looked perfect, but underneath the rubber grip, the plastic was broken. No matter what I tried, it wouldn't fulfill its purpose.

Do you ever feel like something is broken that's keeping you from having the kind of structure leading to spiritual health? Reread the opening passage (2 Peter 1:3). What is the source of the power leading to spiritual health? *God's divine power (Knowledge)*

It's easy to say God is the answer but look at the verse again. The Bible says God has granted us EVERYTHING we need for life and godliness through true knowledge. When we think of knowledge, we look at facts and information stored in our minds.

What is the biblical meaning of knowledge or to know? In the King James Version of the Bible, Genesis 4:1 says, "And Adam knew Eve, his wife, and she conceived." Why did the word "know" mean an intimate relationship between husband and wife in 1611 when the King James Version was translated?

The word *know* means more than just the accumulation of facts. Since it includes the concept of experience, we could see it as gaining understanding through experience and truth. The key to life and godliness is knowledge of Christ or experiencing God. Effective structures include those systems that help us to know God.

As we ascertain His truth in our experience with Him, and His power is unleashed, effective structures will come. Spiritual disciplines are essential, but the disciplines are avenues; knowing God is the destination. Effective structures help us know God and live in His power.

The foundation of spiritual health will be our connection with God through our inner lives. We can't just know the Holy of Holies exists or that we need to have a personal relationship with God. We must *have* a personal relationship with God. It's not enough to talk about our inner life with God. We must first *have* one.

Prayer and Bible reading become mechanisms we use in every structure, along with other spiritual disciplines, but we must use them effectively in order to connect to our Creator. When we read the Bible, our goal must be to encounter God in the Scriptures. When we pray, our objective must be to talk to our Savior and listen to His promptings in our hearts.

Think about how Scripture and prayer strengthen your close relationships with other Christian friends (I referred to these relationships as the "Holy Place" in yesterday's reading). How can you encounter God as a group through the Word? How can you connect to God in prayer with your close Christian friends? Don't be satisfied with the only time you pray in your group being at the start or end your meeting. That's not the purpose of prayer. The purpose of prayer is to encounter God.

Think about the last two structures I mentioned yesterday symbolized by the outer court and the area outside the tabernacle. They represent the church as a whole and the world that doesn't know Christ. How do spiritual disciplines, including Bible reading and prayer, impact your relationship with your church and unbelievers?

_____

_____

In 2 Peter 1:4, Peter wrote about becoming partakers of God's divine nature. He tells us that because our goal is God's nature

(Christlikeness), we must apply diligence by stringing together several objectives. Read 2 Peter 1:5-7 and underline these objectives.

I want you to see things God tells us to add to our lives and to know we must do so with *diligence*, careful and persistent work or effort. If we want the structures of our lives to develop spiritual health and lasting fruit, we must work diligently to see that those goals are met. God's given us His power. He is at work in you and me, but He also calls us to respond with diligence.

> ### 2 Peter 1:5-7
> "Now for this very reason also, applying all diligence, in your faith supply moral excellence, and in *your* moral excellence, knowledge, [6] and in *your* knowledge, self-control, and in *your* self-control, perseverance, and in *your* perseverance, godliness, [7] and in *your* godliness, brotherly kindness, and in *your* brotherly kindness, love."

Look at the next verse (2 Peter 1:8): "For if these *qualities* are yours and are increasing, they render you neither useless nor unfruitful in the true knowledge of our Lord Jesus Christ."

What does this passage say these qualities should be doing in your life?

_____

_____

Because these increasing qualities render you neither useless nor unfruitful in the knowledge of Jesus, it means you are useful and fruitful in your knowledge of Christ (remember the meaning of knowledge).

Think about the four areas that define the spiritual structure of your life symbolized by The Tabernacle. We carry out God's mission through these areas, and He shapes our character to be like Christ.

- The Holy of Holies - our inner life and connection with Christ.

- The Holy Place - our intimate, spiritual connection to a few close Christian friends.
- The Outer Court - our covenant connection with the Body of Christ, the Church.
- The World - our connection to and fulfillment of God's mission with unbelievers.

It's our responsibility to pursue effectiveness in these four areas, but effectiveness doesn't come automatically. It requires diligence. You'll apply diligence through spiritual disciplines in each of these structural areas, which will lead to spiritual health.

Effectiveness doesn't mean we were diligent with certain principles on one day of our spiritual journey. This diligence must be daily. In *Restoring Your Spiritual Passion*, Gordon MacDonald wrote, "Yesterday's spiritual passion cannot be today's inner energy." [1] Just because we're effective today doesn't guarantee effectiveness tomorrow. Diligence requires daily attention.

No one wants methodical structures that make no difference. We want effective structures that fulfill God's purpose for now and eternity.

Personal Reflection

- What is your reaction to the truth God's power has already granted you everything you need for godliness? Are you living a godly life? A spiritually healthy life? *I hope s*
- How do you see diligence in your life related to your spiritual health? What areas can you improve through diligence? *pray*
- Review the four areas or structures of your life symbolized by The Tabernacle. What are specific steps you can take to be effective in fulfilling God's objectives in those areas? Think of various spiritual disciplines and how you can use them to grow in your faith.

- Write a prayer expressing your desire to be effective and diligent. Tell God you want to be useful and fruitful in your knowledge of Christ.

Lord, help me be useful & fruitful in my Knowledge of Christ. Help me understand this book!

Scripture Memory Verse

1 Peter 1:3 "Blessed be the God and Father of our Lord Jesus Christ, who according to His great mercy has caused us to be born again to a living hope through the resurrection of Jesus Christ from the dead."

Day Twenty-three

Inspiring *Worship*

The dark, warm interior of a small room in the Ukrainian nursing home offered protection from the cool night. My team visited the nursing home that evening to share the gospel and lead the elderly residents in a time of worship. We celebrated Christ through songs and testimonies, and we anticipated God working in this service.

One team member had just begun preaching and sharing God's word when the doors flew open, and a young, disheveled-looking man walked in and began shouting in Ukrainian. We were stunned. I could see apprehension and fear on some of the faces of my team. Did he mean us harm? We had no idea what he was saying.

The man wound down minutes later and stalked back out into the night. Our translator said the man told the group they shouldn't be listening to Christians but should be worshiping ancient Ukrainian gods and returning to the culture of their ancestors.

We continued to share God's word, encourage believers, and present the salvation message to unbelievers. I later pondered the experience and realized the man's interruption dealt with a key question for all of humanity: "Whom are we going to worship?"

This question surrounded Adam and Eve's sin in the Garden. It's the question with which we wrestle every day, and it should be on the forefront of our minds when we gather with believers. Whom are *you* going to worship?

God made us to worship Him, and worship is the ultimate purpose of salvation. Jesus laid down His life and made it possible for us to become people who worship the one true God. Worship is a priority, but we fail to understand it's meaning. William Temple, the former Archbishop of Canterbury, gave this detailed definition of worship many years ago:

Worship is the submission of all our nature to God. It is the quickening of conscience by His holiness; the nourishment of mind with His truth; the purifying of imagination by His beauty; the opening of the heart to His love; the surrender of will to His purpose—and all of this gathered up in adoration, the most selfless emotion of which our nature is capable and therefore the chief remedy for that self-centeredness which is our original sin and the source of all actual sin. Yes —worship in spirit and truth is the way to the solution of perplexity and to the liberation from sin. [1]

The fourth chapter of John records the story of Jesus' encounter with the woman at the well. In that conversation, He shared what one writer called one of the strongest statements on worship in the New Testament.

For the woman, worship took place on a mountain, and for the Jews, it took place in Jerusalem. Jesus said a time was coming when worship wouldn't happen in specific geographic locations or earthly temples (Jn 4:21).

> **John 4:23**
>
> "But an hour is coming, and now is, when the true worshipers will worship the Father in spirit and truth; for such people the Father seeks to be His worshipers."

Read Jesus' comment about authentic worship in John 4:23. Consider his emphatic statement describing true worship. The fact He used the word *true* indicates false worship is an option and even a probability for many. Is it possible your worship has ever been inauthentic?

What did Jesus mean when he said true worship is in spirit and truth?

_____

_____

Jesus emphasized authentic worship will come out of a relational connection with God (spirit) and be rooted in the biblical revelation of God's nature and activity (truth). Real worship will connect with our emotions (spirit) and intellect (truth). Is it any wonder the Psalmist wrote, "Bless the Lord, O my soul, and all that is within me bless His holy name" (Psa 103:1)?

As followers of Jesus, our spirits connect with God's Spirit, so worshiping in spirit also means He has redeemed us, forgiven our sin, and restored our relationship with our Heavenly Father. Jesus has given us hope, filled our hearts with attributes of His presence, and set us free from the bondage of sin. Because I am born again, redeemed by the blood of the Lamb, I place my mind's attention on the will of God, and my heart's affection is on His glory.

Paul tells us our bodies are temples of the Holy Spirit, and the person who joins himself to the Lord is one with Him (1 Cor 6:17). It is in this unity we know God. In our hearts, He has become Lord and Savior, and we worship and live in the presence of Him who sits on the throne.

In John 14:6, Jesus said, "I am the way, the Truth, and the life." How does this verse connect to His statement to the woman at the well about worshiping in truth?

Jesus is The truth
_____

Truth is not just a concept or principle. Truth is a person, and He is the Son of God. True worship will be Christ-centered. In John 17:17, Jesus prayed for His church, "Sanctify them in the truth; Your Word is truth." What role does the Scripture play in authentic worship?

_____

_____

Paul wrote we are to become living and holy sacrifices, which is our reasonable service of worship (Rom 12:1). Worship is not just singing; it's also living. Everything can be done for God's glory as an expression of personal worship. By His resurrection power within us, we become living sacrifices when we offer ourselves to Him. Jesus said we are to take up our crosses, follow Him, and deny ourselves daily (Lk 9:23). Our worship becomes a daily walk of spiritually offering ourselves to God for His purposes.

Do you have a time each day when you acknowledge God as Lord of your heart and offer yourself to Him as a living sacrifice? If not, why don't you?

Many things in our lives call for a sacrifice of self. Jobs, gadgets, addictions, pleasures, friends, entertainment, wealth, and many other things scream for our attention every day, but God calls us to the sacrifice of taking up our crosses and following Jesus.

Have you ever been drawn away or tempted to offer yourself as a sacrifice for something or someone other than God? Describe your experience in the space provided.

———————————————————————

———————————————————————

For many, worship has fallen into a kind of spiritual consumerism. They don't believe it is good worship if it doesn't meet their needs or make them happy. It's a kind of worship centered on how I want to feel and what I want to hear. In Romans 12, Paul gave us direction for something entirely different. Instead of being a consumer, we become a sacrifice. Instead of receiving something, we become givers, but through giving, we find life.

When King David went to offer a sacrifice to God, he commented he would not offer something that had not cost him something (2 Sam 24:24). Jesus said it this way, "For whoever wishes to save his life will lose it, but whoever loses his life for My sake will find it (Mt 16:25)." Does your worship cost anything? How can personal or corporate worship include sacrifice?

———————————————————————

God made us and redeemed us to be worshipers. Bruce Leafblad called worshiping God our greatest priority. A. W. Tozer referred to it as the missing jewel. Is it possible worship, your greatest priority, is a missing jewel? Is true worship a missing jewel in the church today? What will you do to experience authentic worship today and on Sunday when you gather with other believers?

Personal Reflection:

- Is there anything between you and God that keeps you from offering yourself as a living sacrifice?   *Maybe – my business*
- Have you ever felt like a consumer instead of a worshiper? *No*
- What do you think Jesus meant when he said, "Whoever loses his life for my sake will <u>find it</u>"?   *Heaven waits*
- Do you consider serving in your church worship?
- Write a prayer expressing your desire to experience true worship. Ask God to show you changes you need to make so worship is the *found* jewel in your life and church.

Lord please help me to experience TRUE worship. Show me the changes I need to worship is the found jewel in your life & church

Day Twenty-four

Inspiring Worship

Now when Solomon had finished praying, fire came down from heaven and consumed the burnt offering and the sacrifices, and the glory of the LORD filled the house. ² And the priests could not enter the house of the LORD because the glory of the LORD filled the LORD'S house. ³ All the sons of Israel, seeing the fire come down and the glory of the LORD upon the house, bowed down on the pavement with their faces to the ground and they worshiped and gave praise to the LORD, saying, "Certainly He is good, certainly His faithfulness is everlasting."

2 Chronicles 7:1-3

John followed in his father's footsteps as a sailor, but after being discharged from the Royal Navy, he was assigned to a ship that would be filled with slaves. It took a hard man with a hardened heart to work in such conditions, and John was such a man.

The crew and captain began tiring of John's contemptible attitude, and they decided to leave him behind with a slave trader in West Africa. After being enslaved for three years, he found freedom once again. Instead of embracing God and Christianity, however, he turned once again to the slave trade.

In giving account of his experiences, John Newton said, "[I was] once an infidel and libertine, a servant of slaves in West Africa."[1]

John Newton found Christ while in a raging storm at sea, and God completely changed his life. In 1780, he joined William Wilberforce and others to stop slave trading in England and wrote what most people consider the most beloved and well-known hymn in America: "Amazing Grace." The hymn continues to speak to hearts around the globe. How has this song inspired you?

God's grace is for me &
I thank Him every day for it!

What is inspiring worship? We often connect the concept to an emotional experience that brings tears or laughter, but God offers something more profound. Inspiring worship doesn't happen as a result of ritual or style. It's not routine or lifeless. Authentic worship takes us to a deeper experience with God that is powerful, thrilling, and enjoyable. It sometimes results in brokenness over sin or celebration over God's goodness, but in the end, real worship impacts our lives.

When we experience authentic worship that connects us to the heart of God, our relationship with Him is strengthened, our community connection is enhanced, and our sense of mission is enlightened. In short, our lives are changed.

Inspiring worship always comes from the source of worship, the Holy Spirit in our hearts. Jesus said our words reveal what is in our hearts (Mt 12:33), and you can see that truth in the words of John Newton's hymn. God turned John Newton's words of cursing into words of praise. If our hearts are right with God, we can worship with words of thanksgiving, praise, and adoration.

God is the initiator of all that happens between Him and humanity. The Bible says He first loved us, called us, paid the price for us, and made a covenant with us. He is the One who is seeking worshipers who worship Him in spirit and truth (Jn 4:23-24). Our praise responds to God's powerful work in both creation and salvation. The soul that has experienced Christ wants to exalt Him through adoration. How has the work of God in your heart inspired you to worship Him?

He loved me first & He sent His Son to die on the cross to save me from my sins

Inspiring worship is offering something back that God has given us. Some may think God needs our help by using hype or some other means to create exciting worship. No! God is complete in Himself and doesn't need our buildings, videos, songs, musical skills, or artistic skills. God has invited us to join Him, and we may offer all these things to Him, but we know that He is the creator of it all.

God gave Bezalel and Oholiab the skill to make beautiful creations with gold and silver. He gave them the ability to teach others to make the artifacts God designed for worship in the Tabernacle (Ex 35:30-35). God gave them the ability to do what He commanded, and He will do the same for you if you trust in Him and exercise faith. He gave King David skillful hands to perform on the harp (2 Sam 16:22-23). If God says make a joyful noise, He will give you the ability to praise Him with sound. He has given us all something we can offer back to Him.

What has God given you to offer to Him in worship?

Giving, teaching, & praising Him

Inspiring worship is experiential and requires God's presence. If God is not present, there is no worship. Jesus reminds us when two or more gather in His name, He is there. The Word tells us God is present where people are praising Him, and He is enthroned on the praises of His people (Psa 22:3).

In the book of Revelation, we read where elders lay down their crowns before Christ (Rev 4:10-11), and we see people from every nation standing and worshiping God (Rev. 7:9). The Bible says, "They cried out with a loud voice, saying, 'Salvation *belongs* to our God who sits on the throne and to the Lamb'" (Rev 7:10). Inspiring worship and celebration can be loud. When a large crowd speaks in worship with one voice, they worship in agreement. Have you ever experienced unity among believers in proclaiming praise to God?

What was the experience like, and how can you encourage other believers to worship in unity?

When I consider what God has done for me, all I can do is thank Him. When I look at the power of God working in me, changing me from the inside out, blessing me with His presence, and answering my prayers, all I can do is praise Him. How can I not rejoice and celebrate Him?

I don't worship with wimpy, lifeless singing. I sing with life and energy because the tomb is empty. When the Body of Christ gathers for worship, we are not singing a funeral dirge because resurrection power is working through every aspect of the experience. God's Word is being sung and preached, and we are being changed. The chains of our bondage are falling off, and the joy of knowing Christ has worked powerfully in us.

As I worship, I'm reminded of how Jesus came into my life, and I'm looking forward to greater things ahead because of His promises. His promises are real. How can I not worship and praise my God? Worship is emotional, but emotion alone is not our goal. We are seeking God, and we will find Him when we seek Him with all our hearts (Jer 29:13). Inspiring worship inspires greater worship and faithful obedience, but inspiration is not something worked up. It's something handed down from a God of grace waiting on us to experience His presence.

Personal Reflection:
- Have you experienced worship that was life-giving, God-focused, and inspiring? Think of a few words that describe your experience. Love of God & Jesus
- Because worship is a way of life and not just an experience, how can your daily activities be turned into expressions of worship? What would change from how you live now?
- How would inspiring worship affect your whole church? What part will you play in helping your church experience authentic worship?
- Write a prayer expressing your desire to experience the kind of worship where you encounter God.

Day Twenty-five

Holistic *Small Groups*

Two are better than one because they have a good return for their labor.
Ecclesiastes 4:9

Helen Keller once said, "Walking with a friend in the dark is better than walking alone in the light." Why would she say walking with a friend is better? We could probably create a list of answers, but the bottom line is God made us for community.

The passage from Ecclesiastes points to the practical side of relationships. Connecting to other people makes sense. Relationships are not just practical; they're also spiritual. I've mentioned the concept of the "one another commands," but why did God command us to be together? Do you suppose it has to do with God knowing us better than we know ourselves? He knows we need community. He hardwired it into our DNA.

Early settlers knew they needed community, but they learned it the hard way. When pioneers first settled their land, they'd put their cabins or sod huts in the middle of their vast landholdings, but they found their mental stability wavered. Settlers learned to build their houses in the corners of their property near other landowners to have a better chance of survival and opportunity for relational connection.

Community is natural because it reflects the nature of God. Do you remember the creation narrative in Genesis 1:27 where God said, "Let us make man in our own image." Notice the plurality of the Godhead. God exists in community with Himself. We call that divine community the Trinity. We reflect God's image best when we stand in community with other believers.

When I use the word "community," I'm not referring to geography. Although you live in a geographic community, I'm referring to a relational community. I'm talking about close relationships where you give and receive, love and are loved, encourage, help, share, and care. It's an intimate relationship where vulnerability is normal, transparency is expected, and honesty is essential.

Read Acts 2:42. The passage says they devoted themselves to four things. What were they?

feeding, fellowship,
eating, praying

Acts 2:42

They were continually devoting themselves to the apostles' teaching and to fellowship, to the breaking of bread and to prayer.

Small groups can be called life groups, community groups, Sunday school, and so forth. The name isn't as important as what happens when they gather. The key elements of a life-giving small group ministry include Bible study, prayer, sharing, encouraging, helping, and serving.

The word translated *fellowship* in Acts 2:42 means sharing deeply together. They shared their lives. We tend to make fellowship something to do with food. Many churches call the place where they eat meals together a fellowship hall. Even though I know better, I still want to make sure food is present any time we get together, but fellowship doesn't have to include food.

Read Acts 2:44-46. Write down a few words that describe the community these early Christians experienced.

Acts 2:44-46

"And all those who had believed were together and had all things in common; 45 and they *began* selling their property and possessions and were sharing them with all, as anyone might have need. 46 Day by day continuing with one mind in the temple, and breaking bread from house to house, they were taking their meals together with gladness and sincerity of heart.

_____

_____

_____

_____

What concepts point to the close community or relationships of these early Christians?

_____

_____

Several words are prominent to me, but one significant phrase is "continuing with one mind." They experienced a oneness from rich fellowship, meaningful prayer, and life-giving Bible study (in their case, the apostles teaching).

According to this passage, where did these early believers meet?

_____from House to house_____

How many were saved that first day? Verse forty-one tells us 3000 people trusted Christ as Savior on the first day, and verse forty-seven says God added to their number daily. These verses underscore how the early church had a double pattern of meeting: large group (in the temple) and small group (from house to house). How many people do you think could have met in a first-century home? Not many.

A small group is not only practical and spiritual, but also it's essential. We have at least thirty-five commands we can't fulfill unless we're together with other believers (the "one another commands"). Some of those commands are difficult to follow with a large group who may not know one another very well. Can you think of one command that requires a closer relationship?

_____

You may have said something like confess your sin to one another. Even the command to encourage one another requires some level of deeper connection. You can encourage people you don't know well in general ways, but when you know someone deeply, you can step into his life, walk with him, and help him through difficult circumstances. That level of connection is encouragement.

The most profound command requiring close relationships is the Hebrews 10:24 command to "stimulate one another to love and

good deeds." You can't obey this command effectively without
trust, vulnerability, and acceptance. Those qualities don't come
from casual relationships. Deep relationships are essential.

Some people thrive off relationships they'll experience in a small
group because this experience relates to their personalities. Here's
an essential truth for those of us who are introverts or loners. You
need community too.

I'm more of an introvert. I love being alone and find I thrive
when I'm by myself. I sometimes don't want to go to small group,
but I feel I must. However, every time I leave my group, I realize
my experience was life-giving. I needed it. I needed them. Being
alone is natural, but being in community is supernatural. Something
eternal, kingdom building, happens when we spend time with a few
close Christian friends studying the Bible, sharing our lives, and
praying together.

Do you meet regularly with a small group of Christian friends? Yes
You will find maturity and ministry happen best in small groups. If
you want to be spiritually healthy, growing in your faith, and producing spiritual fruit, you need to engage regularly with a few Christian friends.   S.S.   God's Girls

Personal Reflection

- Think of an experience you've had of walking with a friend during a dark time. Do you agree with Helen Keller? Was it better
  than walking alone in the light?   Yes

- We often connect eating meals together with fellowship. The
  early church certainly did. Why do we usually include sharing
  meals with fellowship? How can eating together promote
  healthy fellowship?   Time to talk to others

- Think of something you've done with a few close friends that
  has helped you spiritually, but you could not have done it in a
  large group of believers you don't know well.   ?

- God's goal is for you to be a spiritually healthy believer who is being shaped in the image of His Son. How will being a part of a small group help accomplish that goal?

- Write a prayer expressing your desire to be part of a life-giving small group. If you're not in a group, commit to taking steps to gather a group of Christian friends for sharing, serving, prayer, and Bible study.

Holistic Small Groups

But encourage one another day after day, as long as it is still called "Today,"
so that none of you will be hardened by the deceitfulness of sin.
Hebrews 3:13

Years ago, I heard a Zambian proverb: "When you run alone, you run fast, but when you run together, you run far." One of the purposes of being a part of a small group is to run far. Life is not a sprint; it's a marathon.

In 2019, I made it to the 1100-mile point on the Appalachian Trail—halfway. I had hiked from Springer Mountain, Georgia, to a spot south of Pine Grove Furnace State Park in Pennsylvania. It took me many years to accomplish this feat.

Hikers celebrate at a small store in the park by eating a half-gallon of ice cream—the half-gallon challenge. While I sat at a table working on my celebration ice cream, I noticed a runner approaching the store. Trail runners had passed me before, but this guy stopped to talk. He'd run close to fifty miles that day while I'd only hiked about sixteen. I sat eating (making myself sick) while he chatted a moment, declined the ice cream, and left to put in a few more miles before dark. His friends were waiting on him up the trail. This guy had run far.

How do you run far in life? You do so in community, but being in community with others does not mean only attending a small group meeting. The success of small groups happens in response to what goes on in that meeting and how the group experiences meaningful relationships.

As important as small groups (life groups, Sunday school classes, and so forth) are to spiritual health, group experiences only accomplish their purposes when they are holistic. The purposes of these groups are to encounter God together, connect with God and His mission in the world, and help each other be spiritually healthy.

In *Color Your World with Natural Church Development*, Christian Schwarz said a small group should be a microcosm of the church, which means all eight quality characteristics covered in this section should be evident. He wrote, "Holistic small groups should nurture the participants' heads, hands, and hearts."[1] What does this concept mean, and how do you apply it to your journey toward spiritual health?

When Schwarz said small groups should nurture our hearts, he's speaking of our intimate connection with God and with one another. Do you attend a small group? Does your group help you have a deeper relationship with Jesus?

Heart connections with other Christians come more naturally for some, while others find deeper relationships more challenging. Regardless of your personality, you need this kind of relational community which you'll find is essential to your spiritual health. Heart connections with others comes in response to honest and transparent conversation, intercessory prayer for one another, prayer together about general issues, laughing and maybe crying together, and doing life together as friends.

2 Corinthians 6:11-13

Our mouth has spoken freely to you, O Corinthians, our heart is opened wide. [12] You are not restrained by us, but you are restrained in your own affections. [13] Now in a like exchange—I speak as to children—open wide *to us also*.

Paul wrote to Corinthian believers about connecting at this level of intimacy. Read 2 Corinthians 6:11-13. How did Paul describe his heart? What is his request to this group?

open wide

How do we open our hearts wide to one another? Paul mentioned in the opening words that he had spoken freely. This comment points to his honesty and openness. If we have a heart connection with other Christians, we've got to be willing to be open.

We tend to live behind a facade that paints a picture of spiritual health and vitality, but in reality, we're all broken. You'll find your group starting to connect at a heart level when someone opens up and becomes vulnerable. Not only will this kind of honesty strengthen the health of your group, but it will also strengthen your own spiritual health.

How do our community groups nurture our heads? This concept points to mental and theological growth. One significant advantage of meeting regularly with a group of Christian friends is the privilege of asking questions, studying the Bible together, and discussing issues in a safe place. Because of the heart connection with our group, we know nothing we say is out of bounds, deemed insignificant, or set aside because of irrelevance.

We need a place to study and discuss the deeper truths of God and living out our faith. It's essential we grow in our theological understanding and discuss what we're learning with our Christian friends. Although we enjoy conversations about sports and family, the deeper discussions about spiritual topics and our understanding of God's Word and its application will grow our faith and strengthen our lives.

You can change your group dynamic by bringing up spiritual topics for conversation. Imagine sitting around a table and eating together, and you bring up a Bible verse related to that week's study. Share what that passage meant to you and ask the group a question that came to your mind. This approach moves spiritual conversation from the realm of the "Bible study moment" to relational conversation and life application.

Holistic groups also connect with our hands. In other words, healthy groups serve together. Serving should be a natural part of our spiritual overflow, and it helps us grow in our faith. Passages like Galatians 5:13 command us to serve one another, and we'll often find we are as much the beneficiaries of our service as those we serve.

While walking to Jerusalem, Jesus reminded his disciples how many Gentiles lorded their authority over others. He used that moment to teach about servanthood. Read Mark 10:43-45

Mark 10:43-45

"But it is not this way among you, but whoever wishes to become great among you shall be your servant; 44 and whoever wishes to be first among you shall be slave of all. 45 For even the Son of Man did not come to be served, but to serve, and to give His life a ransom for many."

What is the pathway to greatness?

Servant hood

What does the word "slave" suggest? What is Jesus' message in verse forty-four?

Jesus modeled service throughout his life and ultimately served the world by giving his life on a cross. When we serve with others in our small groups, we blend our lives to accomplish God's purpose. Our connection to God and the world expands, and we find the roots of our spiritual lives growing deeper into the soil of God's passion for others.

Personal Reflection

- How have your close relationships with Christian friends helped you "run far"?   _Yes_
- Are you actively involved in a small group? Think of ways your group has experienced the three-fold connection of heart, head, and hands. How has that connection helped you grow in your faith?

- Of the three nurturing areas mentioned, which is easiest for your group? Which one fits better into your comfort level? How can you urge your group to experience all three?

- How has your heart, head, and hands connection with other believers grown your spiritual life?

- Write a prayer expressing your desire to experience a close Christian community with a group of believers. Ask God to help you experience all three levels of connection with your group.

|

Day Twenty-seven

Need-oriented *Evangelism*

You will receive power when the Holy Spirit has come upon you; and you shall be My witnesses both in Jerusalem, and in all Judea and Samaria, and even to the remotest part of the earth. Acts 1:8

When you hear the word evangelism, what comes to mind? I think of my first encounter with a street preacher who stood on a corner preaching the gospel to anyone who'd listen. I also think of an evangelist holding us close enough to the flames of hell I could almost feel the heat.

Oddly, I didn't think of myself in fourth grade telling my friend Martin about Jesus and inviting him to church. I also didn't think about a young man sitting at Starbucks with a friend from work quietly talking about the gospel's claims. Methods and styles vary, but evangelism involves building a bridge with the gospel others can walk across to encounter the saving grace of the Lord Jesus.

Like Peter, you may have the gift of public speaking where you can share the gospel with crowds. You may be able to reason with people like the Apostle Paul using philosophy or logic to point them to the biblical truth. Maybe you're like the blind man healed by Jesus who shared his personal story. Maybe your style involves making friends and sharing Jesus and the basics of Christianity through friendship.

Your methods don't matter, but your obedience does. *→ matters*

Reread Acts 1:8 at the top of the page. Do you see the command to be a witness? The disciples understood being witnesses in Jerusalem, Judea, Samaria, and the remotest part of the earth. How would you apply those four areas to your life? *?*

Newhan,

Notice in this passage that sharing the gospel is a command, not a suggestion. It's easy for us to think we should leave evangelism to the professionals or those who have the gift of evangelism. This verse, however, puts the responsibility upon every believer. The text says you "shall" be a witness. In other words, you're a witness regardless. The question is, what kind of witness are you? People are desperate to know the message of hope found only in the gospel. Will you be a faithful, effective witness? *I am Not !*

In Matthew 5:13, Jesus said, "You are the salt of the earth." What did Jesus mean? *It is my "job" to tell*

other about Jesus

Did you say something about salt being a preservative or offering flavor? How does that apply to being a witness?

_____

_____

Read Matthew 5:14-16. What illustration did Jesus use in these verses to describe our role in sharing the gospel? *Be a light shine before all —*

they see our work & Glorify GOD

Matthew 5:14-16

"You are the light of the world. A city set on a hill cannot be hidden; 15 nor does *anyone* light a lamp and put it under a basket, but on the lampstand, and it gives light to all who are in the house. 16 Let your light shine before men in such a way that they may see your good works, and glorify your Father who is in heaven."

Jesus said a city on a hill couldn't be hidden. How does that truth apply to us? The light of Jesus in us will be evident to those watching the way we live. People should see the fruit of the Spirit (Gal 5:22-23) in us, and grace should overflow from our lives. Jesus even said the world would know we are His disciples by how we love one another. When you become a Christ-follower, your life changes. Paul said we became new creatures (2 Cor 5:17). Jesus said you couldn't hide His light in your life, nor would you want to.

Although Christ's light is evident in us, and we should stand out because of our faith, we still need to be prepared to tell others how to become a Christian. Read 1 Peter 3:15.

The context of this verse deals with our relationships and how we connect with people in our society. Think about the admonition to be prepared to give an answer. That's quite a challenge. That preparation would, at least, include being able to tell someone how to repent of their sins and trust Jesus as their Savior. We ought to have a few Bible verses tucked away in our minds that point to four areas:

> **1 Peter 3:15**
>
> "But in your hearts set apart Christ as Lord. Always be prepared to give an answer to everyone who asks you to give the reason for the hope that you have" (NIV).

1) God's purpose for us (eternal life and relationship with Him - John 3:16),
2) our problem (we're all sinners - Romans 3:23),
3) God's provision (He sent His Son to die for us - Romans 5:8),
4) our response (repenting of our sin and submitting to Christ as Lord - Romans 10:9-10).

Can you think of other ways you could be prepared to give an answer to someone who asks about your faith? How to help someone overcome a few barriers to faith would be worth thinking about. Make a list of three possible barriers to becoming a Christian.

No one to tell them about Him

_____

_____

We don't have to get a Ph.D. in philosophy or apologetics to offer a clear witness, and we don't have to know all the answers. God can use us, however, to help people wade through issues that may keep them from saying yes to Jesus. Romans 10:14-15 challenges us to share the good news and adds a quote from Isaiah 52.

> **Romans 10:14-15**
> But how can they call on him to save them unless they believe in him? And how can they believe in him if they have never heard about him? And how can they hear about him unless someone tells them? 15 And how will anyone go and tell them without being sent? The Scriptures say, "How beautiful are the feet of messengers who bring good news" (NLT).

Have you ever thought about your feet being beautiful? They will be if you are a messenger of the gospel's good news.

Personal Reflection   *Sharing my*
                                  Need
- I described several evangelism styles. Which style fits you best? *for*
                                                                     Jesus
- How have you allowed your light to shine? How does that command change how you live each day?

- Make a list of three things you can do to be prepared to give an answer to someone who asks about your faith.

- Write a prayer expressing your desire to be a witness. Are you willing to express a commitment to prepare yourself to share the gospel?

Learn Roman Rd —

Lord, help me be ready to share the Roman Rd and my witness — Make me take your power & not be afraid —

Day Twenty-eight

Need-oriented Evangelism

If I speak with the tongues of men and of angels, but do not have love, I have become a noisy gong or a clanging cymbal. 1 Corinthians 13:1

I would be surprised if you didn't think evangelism would be a characteristic of spiritually healthy Christians and churches. Studies done by Natural Church Development show healthy churches do not simply evangelize; they practice need-oriented evangelism.

We know sharing the gospel is an essential part of evangelism. The Bible is clear Jesus is the only way to salvation (Jn. 14:6), and we enter a personal relationship with Christ only by grace through faith (Eph 2:8-9). Spiritually healthy Christians will be able to communicate this truth with unbelievers and lead them to faith in Jesus.

Sometimes, however, people can't receive a witness because of other interferences. These interferences can come from various places, such as personal failures, physical impairments, or emotional traumas. As growing believers who are indwelt by the Holy Spirit, our natural response to someone in this state is love. If we are going to be spiritually healthy, effective witnesses, we must build our evangelistic efforts on a foundation of love.

If love is not the foundation, then as 1 Corinthians 13:1 says above, we have become only an annoying noise. When I read that passage, I thought of a battery-operated monkey clanging cymbals together—a lot of action and extremely annoying. If we don't care for those who don't know Christ, our motives for evangelism are skewed, and we are missing the first fruit of the Spirit: love. Lacking love for others points to a deeper spiritual deficiency in our hearts.

Love is a barrier breaker. It becomes a true bridge builder that may open a hardened heart previously closed to the gospel's message. Some people are so lonely and broken by life they can't pay attention to an evangelistic witness and may not believe the Word of God. Love and actions that prove we care may lead them to listen to an evangelistic witness.

Read Mark 1:40-42. What were the barriers or interferences keeping this man from becoming a follower?

leperosy

Mark 1:40-42

And a leper came to Jesus, beseeching Him and falling on his knees before Him, and saying, "If You are willing, You can make me clean." [41] Moved with compassion, Jesus stretched out His hand and touched him, and said to him, "I am willing; be cleansed." [42] Immediately the leprosy left him and he was cleansed."

From the scripture, we see Jesus healed the man of his leprosy, but the passage said He was moved with compassion. What did Jesus do that communicated His love?

touched him + cleansed him

When people had leprosy, they became outcasts. Lepers had to leave their families and move outside the city. They spent the remainder of their lives crying out "unclean" every time someone came near. No one approached a leper for fear of catching the fatal disease. The leper spent his final days alone, suffering, and hopeless.

Amid this desperation, Jesus reached out and touched this man. How long had it been since someone touched him? Jesus could have healed the man from a distance. He could have blown on him, waved his hand, or spoken a word. Instead, Jesus touched him. Why? The man *needed* to be touched.

Sometimes before people can listen to the gospel, their needs will have to be met. Imagine how ludicrous it would be to talk about Jesus, the Bread of Life, to someone who hasn't eaten in days. Love demands we first help them find food. Yes, we need to share, but we first need to care.

Think about the story of Zacchaeus found in Luke 19:1-10. Take a moment to read the story. The tax collector knew he had a need, or was curious about Jesus. People in Jericho hated Zacchaeus because they saw him as a thief and a traitor. When he walked down the street through town, no one called his name. No one wanted to spend time with the wealthy little man who'd become rich at their expense.

Yet Jesus walked to the bottom of the tree in which Zacchaeus was sitting and called out his name. Then Jesus did the unthinkable. He said, "Let's have lunch together." Did Jesus want to have lunch with a thief? Through this encounter, Zacchaeus' life was changed but only because Jesus first cared and then shared.

Can you think of people who need Jesus but may have a barrier to hearing the gospel? How can you show them you care?

Chris + family — I have written letters + send tracks (he lives far away) — told him I loved him

Effective, need-oriented evangelism follows a three-fold approach that reflects balance and obedience. It must include caring and sharing. The third element that connects the witness to the power of God and His supernatural working is prayer. If love is the foundation of an effective witness, prayer has to be the footer upon which the foundation is built. As important as a foundation is to a house, the foundation must sit on deep, concrete footers that provide support. The same is true for prayer in the life of spiritually healthy Christians who witnesses to the lost.

Giving a verbal witness is important, but God is the one who saves. Being a witness is a supernatural event where heaven meets earth. Great spiritual battles are being fought for the souls of humanity, and prayer is an essential part of this battle. Prayer opens our minds to the mind of Christ. Prayer helps us develop sensitivity to what God is doing and helps us know how to join God in His work.

You are probably familiar with Paul's teaching about the spiritual armor found in the sixth chapter of Ephesians. Read Ephesians 6:18-20 to see how he concluded this teaching.

Ephesians 6:18-20

With all prayer and petition pray at all times in the Spirit, and with this in view, be on the alert with all perseverance and petition for all the saints, [19] and *pray* on my behalf, that utterance may be given to me in the opening of my mouth, to make known with boldness the mystery of the gospel, [20] for which I am an ambassador in chains; that in *proclaiming* it I may speak boldly, as I ought to speak.

Notice in this passage the repetition of the words "pray" and "all." What does Paul's request for prayer mean for your witness, and how might it affect how you share your faith?

I need prays from other + prayer from me to speak boldly

Personal Reflection

- What would keep a Christian from not caring about someone who doesn't know Jesus? — *fear*
- What ways can you show genuine love and care for people who are not followers of Christ? How should this care precede a verbal witness? *Visit them + share with them*
- Have you ever shared the gospel with an unbeliever? If not, why haven't you? *Yes — but not enough*
- What role should prayer have in your ministry of evangelism? *pray for me + for those I witness to.*
- Write a prayer expressing your desire to have a balanced witness. Ask God to help you show genuine love and build a prayer ministry for the lost.

Day Twenty-nine

Loving *Relationships*

The second is like it, "You shall love your neighbor as yourself."
Matthew 22:39

The religious leaders of Jesus' day sought with bulldog determination to trip Him up, but they couldn't. In Matthew 22, we read of three unsuccessful attempts to trick Him, the final one by an expert in the law who questioned Jesus on behalf of the Pharisees. These leaders probably debated which command was the greatest many times. They'd reduced the law to 365 negative commands and 248 positive ones. I wonder if they thought He'd pick one of 613 and forget the most significant command of the Jewish people connected to the Shema (Deut 6:4)—the call to love God with everything in us (Deut 6:5).

If we asked Jesus what the greatest command was, we wouldn't be surprised to hear Him say, "Love the Lord your God with all your heart, with all your soul, and with all your mind." The eyebrow-raiser happened when He didn't stop with that command. He said the second one is like it. Of course, the second was a call to love our neighbors. What do you think Jesus meant when he said the command to love our neighbors is *like* the command to love God?

Because God loves all —

As if offering a second commandment wasn't enough, Jesus said the whole law and the writings of the prophets depended on these two commands. By this time, these religious leaders must have been dumbfounded. The law and the prophets made up much of the Old Testament. What do you suppose Jesus meant?

We need to love all

Do you see in these two commands Jesus is saying nothing is more important than relationships? The most significant relationship is to love God, but the second command is connected to the first. If you love God, you will love your neighbor as yourself. If you have a relationship problem with your neighbor, you have a relationship problem with God.

The Word of God is filled with passages that give direction on loving others. Ephesians 4:1-3 is one of those passages.

Ephesians 4:1-3
Therefore I, the prisoner of the Lord, implore you to walk in a manner worthy of the calling with which you have been called, 2 with all humility and gentleness, with patience, showing tolerance for one another in love, 3 being diligent to preserve the unity of the Spirit in the bond of peace.

What qualities should be evident in our love for one another?

humility, gentleness tolerance, patience

Did you pick up on the fact our relationships should reflect our calling to be followers of Jesus? In other words, humility, gentleness, patience, and tolerance are an overflow of God's Spirit living in us. These words make me think of the fruit of the Spirit listed in Galatians 5:22-23.

Why would God command us to be diligent in preserving the unity of the Spirit? Do you suppose unity within the Body of Christ may be under attack? The fact that we *can* maintain unity means unity is a choice we make every day. *No*

Do you find it difficult to be unified with other believers? Being unified with some friends is easy but being unified with others may be a challenge. Our struggle reminds me of a short poem I heard years ago:

To live above with those we love, that will be grace and glory.
To dwell below with those we know, well, that's another story.

Ephesians 4:25-27 offers additional teaching and commands to strengthen our relationships. Paul gives four directives that assist in having strong relationships with our Christian friends. Underline them in the passage.

Have you ever considered your attitude toward others as being something that gives the devil an opportunity to advance his cause? What opportunities are we giving him?

gossip, upset by them

> **Ephesians 4:25-27**
>
> Therefore, laying aside falsehood, speak truth each one *of you* with his neighbor, for we are members of one another. 26 Be angry, and *yet* do not sin; do not let the sun go down on your anger, 27 and do not give the devil an opportunity.

We could make a long list of Satan's opportunities when our relationships aren't intact. We could be destroying testimonies, keeping others from faith in Christ, stealing Christian joy, or hindering spiritual fruit.

In John 17:23, we read where Jesus prayed for unity in the Church. He said we'd be "perfected" or "completed" in unity. What could He have meant? He said our unity leads to spiritual maturity. Have you ever thought your relationships with other people would impact your relationship with God? Have you considered your relationships would affect your spiritual health?

He also said the world would know God the Father sent Him and loved them. Think about that statement. The way we love one another gives evidence to the world Jesus is the Messiah, the Savior of the world, and that God loves them. If we don't have strong relationships with other believers, our witness is tarnished, and God's mission is subverted.

Strong relationships are sometimes difficult to maintain. It's easy to get offended or do something or say something that has a profound, negative impact on another person. Close relationships are like two porcupines in love— someone's going to get hurt. The question is what will we do with that hurt?

God gives us additional instructions to strengthen relationships in Ephesians 4:32, "Be kind to one another, tender-hearted, forgiving each other, just as God in Christ also has forgiven you." This passage is a command, which means it's doable. Kindness is a choice. Forgiving one another is done in response to the fact God has forgiven us.

We want to be spiritually healthy, but the quality of our relationships will have an impact on our level of spiritual health. Because God gives us many commands about strengthening and repairing relationships, we can confidently say He puts the ball in our court. In other words, He tells us always to take the initiative to make a relationship stronger.

Have you ever nurtured a broken relationship? It's not fun. What could you have done to repair it? The way we love others is a billboard advertising how God loves the world.   *apologize
love them*

Personal Reflection

- Do you find Jesus' command to love our neighbors as ourselves challenging? Why do you think He said we should love others the same way we love ourselves? *We should love ourselfs*
- When God commands us to strengthen our relationships, who benefits most from those commands? *Us*
- How do strong relationships build spiritual strength in your life?
- Write a prayer expressing your desire to have strong relationships. If you are struggling in a relationship, ask God to help you deal with the issues so that relationship can honor and represent Him to the world.

Scripture Memory Verse

Philippians 1:6 "*For I am* confident of this very thing, that He who began a good work in you will perfect it until the day of Christ Jesus."

Loving Relationships

Above all, love each other deeply, because love covers over a multitude of sins. 1 Peter 4:8

Josh pressed the doorbell and knew Rick wouldn't be happy to see him.

The front door opened, and Rick dropped his head and looked at the floor. "What are you doing here? I told you my marriage is over. I'm not going back. I told all of you to accept the facts."

Josh pushed the door open and stepped into the foyer. The other three guys in his men's group had been to see Rick numerous times to talk with him about his affair and let him know they still loved him. Josh heard someone working in the kitchen and knew it wasn't Nancy.

He gripped his friend's shoulder. "Rick, we love you too much to watch you throw your life away, and God loves you too much to give up on you. You know you'll never be happy in this relationship. We won't leave you alone because we care about you and Nancy and the kids."

Rick cleared his throat and brushed away a tear. "Thanks, Josh. Tell the other guys I said thanks."

Josh looked toward the kitchen and back at his friend. "So, what are you going to do?"

"I don't know, Josh. I really don't know."

"I'll continue to pray for you, Rick, and any time you want to get together, you can call me. You can call any of us."

"Thanks." Rick's voice cracked. "I guess deep down, I don't want you guys to give up on me."

Josh patted his friend on the back. "We're not, and we won't."

We all understand the concept of relationships, but spiritually healthy people and churches demonstrate *loving* relationships. Although the conversation above is fictional, I know of a similar true story. The men's group wouldn't give up on their friend, and the friend eventually ended the adulterous relationship. He returned to his wife, and the couple sought counseling. After some time, their marriage was restored, and they are happily married today.

Think about the adjective *loving*. What is the distinction between relationships and loving relationships? *love*

Peter wrote that love covers sin, and the fictional story provides an example of that truth. Love doesn't ignore or condone sin but works to restore the sinner. Real love supports, confronts, helps, forgives, encourages, and restores.

Read Galatians 6:1-2. What are the main messages of this passage?

Galatians 6:1-2

Brethren, even if anyone is caught in any trespass, you who are spiritual, restore such a one in a spirit of gentleness; *each one* looking to yourself, so that you too will not be tempted. ² Bear one another's burdens, and thereby fulfill the law of Christ.

Pay attention to the word "burdens" in verse two. The Greek word in the original text referenced a weight too heavy for one person to carry. Have you ever faced a weight like that? Like Rick in the story, overcoming sin can be a daunting experience to face alone. Real love doesn't abandon.

What law of Christ does bearing one another's burdens fulfill?

Reflect on Matthew 22:39 from yesterday's reading? Loving relationships endure while others do not.

What other qualities can be seen in loving relationships? One familiar scripture passage about love is found in 1 Corinthians 13. It's familiar because many pastors read it during wedding ceremonies and rightly so. However, the passage wasn't initially written for married couples. God led Paul to write it for the Church. The Corinthian church was fussing about true spirituality in a very unspiritual way. Paul straightened them out by helping them process the meaning of loving relationships.

Read 1 Corinthians 13:4-8. Don't think about your spouse or your wedding night as you read it. Think about the people in your small group or church.

1 Corinthians 13:4-8

Love is patient, love is kind *and* is not jealous; love does not brag *and* is not arrogant, ⁵ does not act unbecomingly; it does not seek its own, is not provoked, does not take into account a wrong *suffered*, ⁶ does not rejoice in unrighteousness, but rejoices with the truth; ⁷ bears all things, believes all things, hopes all things, endures all things. ⁸ Love never fails.

Genuine loving relationships require time together and regular demonstrations of kindness. For example, if you love someone in your small group, you'll do more than attend your weekly small group together. You may go to the baseball game together or grill with them in the backyard. You'll probably pray for your friend and text encouraging words when he's facing a challenging experience at work. You'll sacrifice time to help when he's in a pinch.

Spiritually healthy churches are made up of individual healthy Christians who know how to love one another deeply. They are mature enough to confront others and gracious enough to forgive when wronged.

Sadly, I've known Christians who refused to forgive others. In one case, a person attended the early service because the person she hated attended the later service. How can that be? The second great-est commandment is like the first. We've got to love!

Look at Jesus' words in John 13:34-35. According to this pas-sage, what are the results of loving one another? *People will know you love*

> **John 13:34-35**
>
> "A new commandment I give to you, that you love one another, even as I have loved you, that you also love one another. [35] By this all men will know that you are My disciples, if you have love for one another."

Consider relationships you have with others in your church. It's dif-ficult to love everyone deeply if you attend a large church because you don't know everyone, so you may need to narrow your perspective to your small group or Sunday School class. Would you say you demon-strate loving relationships with *Yes* those in your group? Before you an-swer, think of specific ways you show the deep love Peter wrote about. What steps can you take to love those around you more? *Hug them - Pray for them Help them.*

Personal Reflection

- Have you ever been part of a group who *yes* modeled authentic, loving relationships? If so, describe those relationships. If not, how would people in a group like that relate?

- What barriers are keeping you from experiencing loving rela-tionships? Are you willing to overcome those barriers? What must you do?

- What may come to mind when unbelievers think about Chris-tians? Loving relationships? Why or why not? How serious should you be about loving others deeply? *Very serious*

- Write a prayer expressing your desire for loving relationships. You may need to confess you haven't loved others like that but tell God you want to begin now. Ask Him to show you the path to take.

Final Thoughts

We've come to the end of our thirty-day journey, but it's just the beginning of a lifelong focus on your relationship with Jesus. Spiritual health isn't the result of a thirty-day discipline, nor is it the consequence of participating in a particular discipline for one hundred days. Spiritual health results from an ongoing effort to deepen our relationship with Christ and His Church, and it overflows from our lives as we connect to God's mission in the world.

Spiritual health is not like physical health. If you want to be physically healthy, follow this checklist: exercise daily, including cardiovascular exercise, eat a balanced diet low in fat and cholesterol, get plenty of sleep each night, and develop activities to reduce stress. If you follow this list, you will become healthier.

Spiritual health is different because it's tied to a relationship with Jesus. You can't just follow a checklist that results in greater spiritual well-being. It's possible to read your Bible every day, pray regularly, attend church, participate in ministry, and still be far from God. Part of our spiritual health comes from knowing and experiencing God, which is why we spent the first eight days focused on that theme.

Spiritual health is also the result of releasing growth forces that automatically work with spiritual disciplines and eight focused qualities to produce a stronger relationship with Christ and a deeper faith. You must be willing to take the disciplines and activities and use them to encounter God in order to release His power and presence to work in your life. Think relationship not ritual. Think love not legalism.

We also hope you understand the truth that healthy churches consist of healthy Christians. As you grow deeper in faith and stronger in spirituality, you'll find growth doesn't happen in a vacuum. We exist in community, and our growth is never restricted to ourselves. We always bring people along with us on the journey. As you grow healthier, your small group will grow healthier. As small groups deepen their faith, the result upon your entire church will be astounding.

The question you must consider is what will you do next? The objective of this study is not to complete a thirty-day devotional but to develop a spiritually healthy life, a lifelong pursuit.

So, what's next? I suggest several things:

Pursue a daily quiet time with God. You can find numerous resources that will help. I've written a book on basic discipleship called *Following Jesus: A 21-Day Journey*. Another excellent study that will bless your life and strengthen your faith is called *Master Life*. *Experiencing God* is one study that profoundly affected me years ago. God is raising up many Christian authors to create relevant resources that will bless your journey.

Connect with other believers in Christian community. God didn't design you to fly solo. Include several close friends you meet with for prayer, Bible study, ministry, and fellowship. Pray together and play together. God will use your community to deepen your faith and fortify your spirit.

Be intentional about strengthening your church. I'm sure you want to be part of a healthy church. Don't be content with spiritual anemia in your congregation. Meet with your pastors and be part of the solution.

Find your ministry. You cannot have a passionate relationship with Jesus without using your gift in meaningful ministry. Discern your spiritual gift(s) and put it (them) to work.

Pray without ceasing. Years ago, Dr. Jerry Falwell, Sr., said, "Nothing of eternal significance ever happens apart from prayer." I believe it. Pray alone and pray with family and friends. Cry out to God for revival. Surrender and ask for revival in your heart.

Obey the Word of God. Read the Bible, and when God tells you to do something, do it. Start a Bible movement in your church and community. God's Word is our source of truth and our guide for life. Dive deep and mine the spiritual riches.

Remember, just because you may be spiritually healthy today doesn't mean you'll be spiritually healthy tomorrow. Spiritual health is a process, journey, lifestyle, and relationship.

A. W. Tozer said it well: "The impulse to pursue God originates with God, but the outworking of that impulse is our following hard after Him." [1] Follow the impulse and pursue Christ.

A Note from the Authors

Thank you so much for joining us for a thirty-day experience to strengthen your spiritual health. We hope you were impacted by your study and have developed some lifelong habits that will change your life.

Our desire is that you are not only personally affected by your study, but your church will also grow stronger with you. What can you do to transfer these principles to your Christian community?

If this book has been a blessing to you, **will you consider posting a review on Amazon** so others may be encouraged by your journey? Writing a review is a simple task that you can complete in literally seconds, but it can have an eternal benefit in someone's life.

We'd like to offer you a **free resource** to help you study Psalms. You can get your copy by visiting greentreepublishers.com and choose "Free Gift-Psalms." When you download this book, you'll also be joining a group of people who receive periodic newsletters where you'll enjoy Bible study helps and resources that will encourage you along your Christian journey.

May God bless you as you seek Him in the days to come, and may you grow stronger in your faith.

Dan & Tim Riordan
Website: timriordan.com

HOW TO BECOME A CHRISTIAN

The journey of faith begins with a relationship with Jesus Christ. This section is provided to help you enter a personal relationship with the One Who loves you and died so you can obtain a personal relationship with your Creator, eternal life, and lasting security. If asked, many people in the United States would claim to be Christians, but what does it really mean to be a Christian? How does one "cross over" to a life of faith?

We must understand a few truths. One critical thing we need to know is that God made us for relationships, and the number one relationship He made us for is the relationship with Himself. While  God wants a relationship with us, the fact is that deep down in our hearts, we long for a relationship with God. Sometimes we try to fill that longing with all manner of things such as careers, accomplishments, financial success, patriotism, sex, or hedonism. The list could go on. In all our attempts to fill the void in our lives, we come up empty-handed, or maybe I should say "empty-hearted." One philosopher said we have a God-sized void in our hearts without Jesus. If we try to fill the void in our lives with anything other than God, the void will remain just that—a void. Our longing, or our hunger, is for God and God alone.

The Bible teaches that every human being is born separated from God because of sin. Romans 3:23 says, *"For all have sinned and fall short of the glory of God."* A few verses prior to this, the Bible says, *"There is none righteous, not even one"* (Rom 3:10). Our society has tried to hide the reality of sin, but the fact is sin is not only all around us, but it is also all in us.

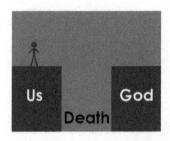

Sin could be defined as missing the mark of God's perfection. It is doing, saying, or thinking anything contrary to the ways and will of God. We are all guilty. We can try to redefine the term or compare ourselves to people of lesser morals, but the bottom line is every human being is born with a nature to do wrong, and we also occasionally, or not so occasionally, chose to sin. One problem we have is that while we are not righteous, God IS righteous and holy. He can have nothing to do with sin, even though He loves the sinner (see Rom 5:8). This creates a great divide between us and God. The natural result of humanity apart from God is death. Romans 6:23 says, *"The wages of sin is death…"* This concept of death is more than just ceasing to have a heartbeat. This "death" means eternal separation from God.

People try to get to God through all manner of means. Most people think if they are good enough, God will give them a pass into heaven. It's almost as if there is a large scale in heaven where all our deeds are weighed. The good deeds are placed on the plate to the right and the bad deeds are placed on the left. If the good deeds outweigh the bad deeds, then we feel as if God is obligated to let us in to His heaven. The Bible says in Isaiah 64:6 *"all our righteous deeds are like a filthy garment,"* and Ephesians 2:8-9 clearly says we are not saved by doing good works: *"For by grace you have been saved through faith; and that not of yourselves, it is the gift of God; not as a result of works, so that no one may boast."*

While God is compassionate, merciful, and gracious, He is also holy, righteous, and just. If God simply gave us a pass and let us into His heaven, He would not be righteous and just. If He sent us all to hell with no hope for eternal life, He would not be gracious. God's answer, and our solution, is Jesus Christ. God sent His Son to die for the sins of the world. John 3:16 says, *"For God so loved the world, that He gave His only begotten Son, that whoever believes in Him shall not perish, but have eternal life."* Jesus paid for our sins with His own life and then rose again from the dead declaring He is indeed God (see Rom 1:4).

God has given to us an option: either we pay for our sins through our own eternal death and separation from God, or we allow Christ's death to pay for our sins as we trust Him as our Savior. In essence, Jesus became our bridge to the Father. Through Jesus Christ, and only through Jesus Christ, we can enter a relationship with our Creator. Jesus said, "*I am the way, and the truth, and the life; no one comes to the Father but through Me.*" Acts 4:12 says of Jesus, "*And there is salvation in no one else; for there is no other name under heaven that has been given among men by which we must be saved.*"

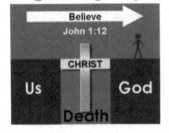

We enter a relationship with God through repentance of our sin and faith in Jesus Christ. Repentance means turning around. Whereas, once we were following our own way and our own desires, to repent means we turn and follow God's way and seek to fulfill His desires. Placing our faith in Jesus means more than just intellectually accepting the facts about Christ's identity and work. The Bible says in James 2:19: "*You believe that there is one God. Good! Even the demons believe that—and shudder*" (NIV). True faith comes as we surrender our lives to Jesus Christ allowing Him to be the King of our heart and the Leader of our life. Romans 10:9-10 says, "*If you confess with your mouth Jesus as Lord, and believe in your heart that God raised Him from the dead, you will be saved; for with the heart a person believes, resulting in righteousness, and with the mouth he confesses, resulting in salvation.*"

Christianity is a choice to surrender to Jesus Christ as the Lord of your life. This is what the word *believe* means in John 1:12. Surrender means totally giving your life into the hands of someone else. Imagine drowning in a lake, and a lifeguard swims out to rescue you. The only way you can be saved from sure death is to quit fighting and surrender to the saving grasp of the lifeguard. Becoming a Christian is not just praying a prayer. It is not just going to church.

It is not just trying to reform your life. Becoming a Christian is turn-ing from sin and self and choosing to follow Jesus as your Sovereign King.

You can express this decision in a prayer as you cry out to God. If you have never done this and would like to, why not bow your head right now and tell Jesus you acknowledge you are a sinner in need of forgiveness. Tell Him you believe He died for you and rose again and ask Him to forgive you for your sin and come into your life. Commit yourself to be a Christ-follower for the rest of your days. Thank Him for His grace and pledge yourself to begin your new life today by seeking to grow as a new believer. I encourage you to do this right now. The Bible says in 2 Corinthians 6:2, *"Behold, now is the acceptable time; behold, now is the day of salvation."*

What's next? While going to church doesn't save you, it sure helps you grow as a Christian. You will build relationships with other Christians who are seeking to grow in Christ and serve God with their lives. You will be encouraged in your faith and will grow in your understanding of the Bible, God's Word. I encourage you to find a Bible-believing church to attend where the Bible is taught, and good, Christian friendships can be enjoyed.

Is there someone who would like to hear of your decision to become a Christian? Why not call them right now and let them know of your new faith? Do you have Christian friends whom you admire? Why not call them right now and ask if you can go to church with them on Sunday? If you do not have Christian friends with whom you can share your decision, simply tell someone close to you. If you already attend a Bible-believing, Bible-teaching church, give your pastor a call, and let him know of your decision to trust Christ as your Savior. I also hope you'll contact me. I'd love to know of your decision and to pray for you as you grow in Christ.

Welcome to the Family of God!

Special thanks to Heather Bible Chapel for assistance with "The Bridge" graphics.

Endnotes

Day Seven:
1. Henry Blackaby and Claude King, *Experiencing God: Knowing and Doing the Will of God,* (Nashville: Lifeway Press, 2007), 142.

Day Fifteen:
1. George Barna, Leaders on Leadership: Wisdom, Advice, and Encouragement on the Art of Leading God's People. (Grand Rapids: Baker Books, 1997), 18.
2. Henry and Richard Blackaby, *Spiritual Leadership: Moving People On To God's Agenda,* (Nashville: Broadman & Holman Publishers, 2001), 20.

Day Seventeen
1. Elizbeth Hopper, "Can Helping Others Help You Find Meaning in Life?" *Greater Good Magazine,* University of California – Berkeley, February 16, 2016, https://greatergood.berkeley.edu/article/item/can_helping_others_help_you_find_meaning_in_life.

2. Katherine B.Hanniball, Lara B.Aknin, Kevin S.Douglas, Jodi L.Viljoen, "Does Helping Promote Well-being in At-risk Youth and Ex-offender Samples," *Journal of Experimental Social Psychology,* Vol 82, May 2019, https://www.sciencedirect.com/science/article/abs/pii/S0022103118304219#!

Day Nineteen
1. Dallas Willard, The Spirit of the Disciplines, (San Francisco: HarperSanFrancisco, 1988), 156.
2. John Ortberg, *The Life You've Always Wanted,* (Grand Rapids: Zondervan, 2002).

Day Twenty-two
1. Gordon MacDonald, *Restoring Your Spiritual Passion,* (Nashville: Oliver-Nelson Books, 1986), 37.

Day Twenty-three:
1. William Temple, *Readings in St. John's Gospel*, First Series (London: Macmillan and Co., 1939), 68.

Day Twenty-four:
1. Grant Piper, "The Incredible True Story of John Newton, the Man who Wrote 'Amazing Grace,'" July 14, 2021, https://grantpiperwriting.medium.com/the-incredible-true-story-of-john-newton-the-man-who-wrote-amazing-grace-2502d215093

Day Twenty-six:
1. Christian Schwarz, *Color Your World with Natural Church Development*, 2nd USA ed. (St. Charles, IL: Church Smart Resources, 2007), 116.

Final Thoughts:
1. A. W. Tozer, *The Pursuit of God: The Human Thirst for the Divine*, (Chicago: Moody Press, 2006), 18.

MORE BOOKS FROM GREENTREE PUBLISHERS

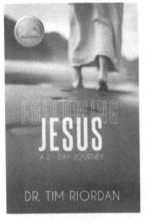

Following Jesus: A 21-Day Journey
By Tim Riordan

Physical growth is automatic; spiritual growth isn't. Since you've become a follower of Jesus, what are you doing to grow in your faith? Some people focus on the event of becoming a Christian and forget the process of following Jesus.

Following Jesus is a guide to help you experience Jesus and grow in your faith. This book was a 2022 Selah Award finalist.

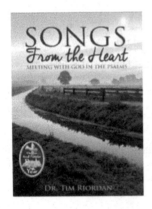

Songs from the Heart: Meeting with God in the Psalms
By Tim Riordan

Songs from the Heart: Meeting with God in the Psalms is a Bible study/devotional on one of the most loved books of the Bible: the Psalms. Join Dr. Tim Riordan as he shares insights on these beloved passages through Bible teaching and storytelling, making personal application to your life. The 2016 Christian Small Publishers Association book of the year.

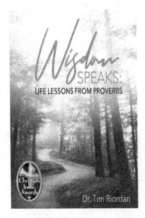

Wisdom Speaks: Life Lessons from Proverbs
By Tim Riordan

Have you ever wished for a "How To" book on life? God has given us one in the book of Proverbs. Join pastor and Bible teacher Dr. Tim Riordan on a journey through this book of wisdom where you study one of the most read books of the Bible. Through Proverbs, wisdom speaks. Are you listening? Chosen for the Christian Indie Award in 2019.

When God Promises
Taking God at His Word will free you
from Worry, Stress, & Fear
By Julie McCoy

This six-week study draws on the experiences of people in the Bible who discovered the power of taking God at His word. As you explore their stories you will learn how trusting God's faithfulness to do what He says will give you victory over worry, stress, and fear.

The Davenport Series
By Judah Knight

Dive into an adventure of scuba diving, treasure hunting, danger and suspense in Judah Knight's exciting series. Meet Jon, Meg, Lacy, Kerrick, and others in this clean and wholesome romantic suspense series that will keep you on the edge of your seat and challenge you to pursue the kind of relationships you've always wanted. Enjoy flinch-free fiction that is safe for the whole family.

Judah Knight was a finalist for 2019 Georgia author of the year.

For more information on any of our publications,
visit greentreepublishers.com.